STRIKE FOR FREEDOM!

STRIKE FOR FREEDOM!
The Story of Lech Walesa and Polish Solidarity

By Robert Eringer

ILLUSTRATED WITH PHOTOGRAPHS

DODD, MEAD & COMPANY · NEW YORK

Frontispiece: A Polish worker

All the illustrations in this book are from United Press International Photo
with the following exceptions: the frontispiece photograph of the Polish
worker, Walesa's boyhood home (p. 41), Corporal Walesa (p. 41), Walesa and
his new wife (p. 42), the two Solidarity newspapers (pp. 44, 45), the hero with
his wife and child (p. 47), and the portrait of a leader (p. 48).

1 2 3 4 5 6 7 8 9 10

48342

Library of Congress Cataloging in Publication Data

Eringer, Robert.
    Strike for freedom!

1. NSZZ "Solidarność" Labor organization)
2. Walesa, Lech, 1943-   I. Title.
HD8537.N783E7 1982   322'.2'0924   82-12978
ISBN 0-396-08065-0

In Memory of EDWARD STANLEY

AUTHOR'S NOTE

This book could not have been possible
without the assistance of a Polish
journalist who must remain nameless.

Contents

Illustrations

STRIKE FOR FREEDOM!

Baltic Sea

Gdynia
Sopot
Koszalin
Gdansk
Elblag

Olsztyn

Szczecin

Torun

Poznam
POLAND
Warsaw

EAST
GERMANY

Lodz

Wroclaw

Czestochowa

Lublin

Krakow

CZECHOSLOVAKIA

Rzeszow

U.S.S.R.

0   100
miles

I.

Martial Law

THREE WEEKS before Christmas 1981, as the people of Poland were bracing themselves for the demanding winter cold and snows of northern Europe, it was becoming increasingly clear that the country was on the brink of economic collapse and that disagreements between Solidarity and the government were reaching the breaking point. A major confrontation was impending and tensions had reached insufferable proportions. It was obvious that *something* decisive was unavoidable.

It came in the early morning hours of Sunday, December 13, 1981, and what occurred meant that the sixteen-month-old struggle by the independent trade union movement called Solidarity and its worker leader, Lech Walesa, to achieve freedom for the people of Poland was brought to a sudden halt by military rule.

Still, the abrupt resolution of the crisis took the country and the world by surprise. As people rose from their beds that Sunday morning, they were startled to learn over their radios and television sets that a "state of war" had been declared within Poland by the Communist Party leader, General Wojciech Jaruzelski, and that martial law had been implemented. Throughout Warsaw and other major Polish cities tanks and armored vehicles of the Polish Army had taken up positions to quash any antigovernment rebellions. With army troops at their posts, it was announced that a military "Council of National Salvation" had been created, that the Council had "suspended" the ten-million-member Solidarity union, that the freedoms the union had won were canceled, and that the Council was now in command of Poland.

If nothing else, it had to be admitted that the government's actions were brilliantly staged. There had been no hint of the massive repression. Hours before Jaruzelski's appearance on the television screens, telephone lines had been cut in Gdansk while Solidarity leaders held a Saturday night meeting to formulate tough new demands. But few thought the cutting of the lines was ominous for Solidarity. No one truly expected martial law, or at least not so soon. If the military were to take action, union leaders reasoned, it would come four days later on December 17 when a day of national protest was planned by Solidarity.

They were caught off their guard, for even as they wound up their meeting, Jaruzelski's soldiers were taking charge of all state communication systems. At 11:45 P.M. an Italian comedy film on television was abruptly interrupted and the airwaves shut down for the night.

At midnight the ZOMO, Poland's antiriot police, moved in on the five-story structure on Mokotowska Street, a former schoolhouse, which served as Solidarity's Warsaw headquarters. They quickly sealed off the site by blockading its two approaches and ransacked the building of documents. (Authorities later claimed the confiscated papers proved Solidarity was planning to seize power, but they fell short of providing evidence.) The ZOMO smashed telex equipment and water pipes, flooding much of the building. More than two dozen Solidarity employees were seized in the raid.

At 2:00 A.M. Solidarity leaders were awakened and apprehended at the Krapolinski Hotel in Gdansk where they were staying during their weekend meeting. (Officers of the secret police had quietly booked themselves into adjacent rooms in preparation for the coup.)

Armed with metal truncheons, five officers of ZOMO arrived at Walesa's Gdansk apartment door at midnight and awakened the startled union leader's wife. "Madam, tell your husband that we have come to take him to General Jaruzelski," one of the officers called to Mrs. Walesa. She refused to open the door.

Walesa, clad in pajamas, appeared and shouted to the officers to bring the local party first secretary to the scene. The ZOMO agents departed and returned one hour later with the first secretary, whom Walesa permitted to enter the apartment.

Satisfied that Jaruzelski required his presence, Walesa dressed, kissed his wife goodbye, and was driven to a waiting military helicopter for a flight to Warsaw. He was met in the Polish capital by Stanislaw Ciosek, Poland's Minister for Trade Unions, and was then driven to a villa at Chylocyke, near Warsaw. His internment, as a "house guest," had begun. (Ciosek later said that Walesa had behaved like a man in shock.)

At 6:00 A.M. General Jaruzelski addressed the stunned nation and formally declared martial law. "Our country is on the edge of abyss," he solemnly intoned. He requested that all Poles remain calm, and work together toward solving the country's food and economic problems. "There is one thing I want— peace," Jaruzelski continued. "We have come out of this crisis by ourselves . . . history would never forgive us if we failed."

The twenty-three-minute speech was repeated over the radio every hour throughout the long day, followed by the national anthem. Meanwhile, the lines of all telexes and telephones, 3,439,700 of them, were cut. International travel was halted; all flights by LOT, the Polish national airline, were cancelled, all borders and air space closed. Poland literally had been separated from the rest of the world as Polish troops, tanks, and armored vehicles took up dominant positions throughout the country. Jaruzelski's strategy was well planned, his military presence total. Poland's railways, seaports, airports, transport systems, and communications, including post offices, were effectively "militarized." Censorship was legalized, universities were closed, and by noon Sunday over two thousand Solidarity activists had been rounded up and detained. In addition, almost forty former high-ranking Communist Party officials, including two former party leaders, were arrested and confined to their homes under guard; Jaruzelski's "concession," some whispered.

Under brilliant winter sunshine, people wandered in a daze around Warsaw's glistening snow-covered streets. "There was a look of utter incomprehension on most faces," said one eyewitness. Freshly printed posters pasted to walls spelled out the suspension of their freedom, and to drive the point home, armored personnel carriers roamed the city's roads. Soldiers in fours and fives patrolled every street corner, wielding naked bayonets. It was a state of siege; Poland had declared war on itself; its military occupied the country.

"Don't you think this is childish?" asked one old woman of the young soldiers on patrol.

The soldiers, many oblivious to what was going on, directed traffic, inspected identification cards, now required of all Poles, and searched passing cars and vans for Solidarity literature.

Outside what had been Solidarity's headquarters, a large crowd of protestors baited the police with jeers of "Gestapo," and the police responded with bursts of ice-cold water shot from fire hoses.

By midafternoon Warsaw's sad streets were deserted of all but military personnel, and all traces of Solidarity's existence—wall posters, slogans, etc.—were wiped clean. The capital was calm except for snowball fights, which broke out sporadically between youths and soldiers.

Archbishop Jozef Glemp, the Polish primate, delivered a sermon pleading for Poles not to fight Poles. In Rome, Pope John Paul II, the first man in the West to learn of martial law (he was phoned the news at 1:00 A.M. by Poland's ambassador to Italy), pleaded to his homeland for a peaceful solution.

Throughout Monday the new military council, which consisted of fourteen generals, one admiral, and five colonels (with Jaruzelski at the helm), announced strict new measures—sixty-one decrees in all. A 10:00 P.M. to 6:00 A.M. curfew was declared, and all publications and political activities were banned, as were all public gatherings, except for religious services. Poles were barred from leaving the country and ordered to stay away from border regions; their passports were invalid. All foreign currency accounts were frozen. Possession of a shortwave radio was made illegal, all private sale of gasoline was outlawed, and the sale and consumption of alcohol was prohibited. "Militarization" was extended to include oil refineries, power plants, and coal mines, and military broadcasters in full uniform replaced television and radio journalists. (All journalists who held membership in Solidarity were later sacked.) The only newspaper allowed to continue was the army's own *Zolnierz Wolnosci.*

Passive resistance and strikes began on Monday. Industrial production was far below normal as factories lay idle. In Gdansk, the Baltic birthplace of Solidarity, thirteen thousand strikers occupied the Lenin Shipyard and refused to work. The large steelworks factories in Katowice, Cracow, and Warsaw were also at a standstill. Steelworkers turned up for their shifts, but did not work. A large sign at the Katowice steel mill summed up the strikers' feelings: "Jaruzelski Traitor to the Workers." Miners in the coal-rich Silesian district were more radical. They barricaded themselves underground in their mines and threatened to detonate explosives.

The number of strikes totaled 261, in eight provinces. Poland was not producing and Jaruzelski was clearly worried. He attempted to recruit Walesa's assistance to calm the angry workers, but Walesa refused a meeting with Jaruzelski unless Archbishop Glemp could be present. Glemp, in turn, refused to see Jaruzelski unless Walesa could be present, and Jaruzelski would not agree.

When Walesa was asked late Monday night to appear

on national television and appeal for order, he refused to take any decision until permitted to consult with his entire Solidarity presidium, most of whom were also detained. "You will have to cut my body into a thousand pieces first," he reportedly told his captors.

In the early hours of Tuesday morning, riot police decked out in helmets and shields raided the Huta steel mill, Warsaw's largest factory and Solidarity stronghold, and arrested twenty union leaders. At noon troops and armored vehicles smashed through the Lenin Shipyard gates in Gdansk and dispersed strikers with tear gas. Over three hundred persons were injured in the pitched battles fought throughout the day.

In the capital, police stormed the University of Warsaw and dragged away dissident professors and Solidarity activists. A similar assault was made on the Academy of Arts and Sciences, where over a hundred members were arrested.

Official news broadcasts spoke reassuringly of order. "On the whole, the country is calm," reported one such bulletin. "Factories report a high turnout of work forces." But information spread, by word of mouth and through Solidarity couriers, of widespread resistance. Walesa himself managed to smuggle a message to the Council of Polish Bishops:

1. Don't let us be crushed.
2. Support mass strikes in the major industries and passive resistance in small businesses.

3. In the event of the use of force by the army try to avoid the shedding of blood.
4. Let us unite. Let us show that our union is alive and can still act.

As Pope John Paul II publicly appealed on Wednesday to Poland's new military rulers for the resumption of negotiation with Solidarity, clashes between workers and the security forces grew more violent.

In Gdansk, riots continued. Using tear gas and water cannon, troops restored order there by late evening, though at the cost of several hundred injured.

At the Wujek coal mine in Katowice disaster struck. Police mounted an offensive and panicked when confronted by strikers armed with picks, chains, and bricks. They opened fire, killing seven strikers and seriously injuring over three dozen others. Almost eleven years to the day since the 1970 riots, Pole had killed Pole.

The following day, several thousand demonstrators were set upon by antiriot squads after they had gathered at Warsaw's Victory Square to light candles and sing hymns near a cross commemorating the late Cardinal Wyszynski. Many were injured as police chased the offenders through the narrow, cobblestoned streets of Warsaw's Old Town, and even into churches.

Widespread resistance continued throughout Poland, coupled with food hoarding. Workers would turn up at factories, but only pretend to work—what they called an "Italian strike."

The military council stepped up its enforcement of "normalization" with tougher warnings and many more arrests. Polish broadcasts blamed the killings in Katowice on "irresponsible provocateurs," but Jaruzelski was privately said to be in deep despair over the spilled blood.

The Soviet Union and Eastern European countries hailed Jaruzelski's actions as overdue. Western nations were aghast at the coup, but had great trouble concerting their protest. In the United States, President Reagan ordered an immediate halt to all American food shipments to Poland, and he publicly accused Soviet leaders of interfering in Poland's affairs. It was pointed out that Marshall Viktor Kulikov, the Soviet commander of Warsaw Pact forces, had been in and out of Poland several times during the weeks preceding martial law. The Kremlin, some believed, had issued Poland's leaders with an ultimatum: either you do it, or we will.

But the imposition of martial law was overall a Polish attempt to solve a Polish problem. The military Council of National Salvation was not, as some suggest, a puppet government. Indeed, for the first time in Eastern Europe, the military had wrested political power away from Communist Party management. It occurred under extraordinary circumstances, but nonetheless it was a reality that certainly worried the Kremlin.

On Sunday, December 20, in an expression of solidarity "with Lech Walesa," the Polish ambassador to Washington, career diplomat Romuald Spasowski, requested and was immediately granted political asylum in the United States for himself and his family. "A state of war has been imposed against the Polish people," he declared. "I cannot be silent." (He was soon followed by Poland's ambassador to Japan, Zdzislaw Rurarz.)

Christmas 1981 in Poland was a grim affair, its people demoralized. With telephone lines cut and harsh travel restrictions imposed, many families spent Christmas worrying anxiously about the fate of relatives. Conscripted soldiers were ordered to remain on duty, but the curfew was lifted Thursday night so that Poles could attend Christmas Eve midnight mass.

Shoppers stood freezing in long queues at stores trying to buy carp, the traditional Christmas Eve dinner, and what few Christmas treats were available. Scrawny Christmas trees were in short supply. An extra place was set at every Christmas table to symbolize the absence of a detained friend or relative.

As many as twelve hundred Poles—Solidarity leaders, journalists, artists, writers, and intellectuals—spent an unfestive Christmas interned under bleak conditions at forty-nine camps around the country, the largest of which was located on the Hel peninsula near Gdansk. There were reports that three hundred detainees were kept outside in temperatures below freezing and doused with water every hour.

Over a thousand striking coal miners in Silesia, southern Poland, spent Christmas underground in occupation of their mines. It was ironic that after splitting up countless families through travel restrictions and internment, the Polish authorities directed broadcasts at the miners suggesting that Christmas was a time to spend with one's family. But the miners would not be lured out, not even for Christmas.

Walesa spent a lonely Christmas without his family, sealed off in detention at the heavily guarded headquarters of the Polish Army general staff in Warsaw. He ended a two-day hunger strike on Christmas day.

On Christmas Eve millions of candles flickered in the windows of homes around the world—including the White House and Pope John Paul II's private apartment—as a symbol, announced President Reagan, "of our solidarity with the Polish people."

By New Year's Eve, the Silesian coal miners' strike had ended. Amid heavy snowfalls and icy-cold conditions, the "normalization" process had begun to take hold; an announcement of sharp price increases for raw materials and tighter meat rationing met little organized opposition. If Solidarity had ever devised a national contingency plan, it did not work.

On the streets of Warsaw there was still some amazement over why martial law had been imposed. Many Poles did not believe Jaruzelski's claim that there was no other option. One Polish sociologist felt the authorities did not properly understand the nature of the mass movement. The authorities, he said, thought that by seizing the movement's leaders they could end it all.

"The winter is yours," read a slogan on a Gdansk

shipyard wall, "but the spring will be ours."
When that spring will arrive no one knows.

———

What follows is a quick review of Poland's history and
the story of sixteen months of Solidarity—a study in
courage and determination, the story of Lech Walesa,
an unemployed shipworker, the son of a village carpenter, who boldly declared a strike and became an international hero.

2.

Russia to the East, Germany to the West

THE STRUGGLE of the people of Poland to live as a group within a nation free from outside interference or domination is a story of resistance to other countries eager to carve up slices of Polish territory for themselves. Without question the two countries most eager for free helpings of Poland have been Russia on the east and Germany on the west.

Poland was created as a nation under Prince Mieszko in 966, the year it was recognized by the Vatican as a Christian kingdom. Before then, Poland had been inhabited by several Slavic tribes, the most powerful of which were the Polane. These tribes were united against the Germanic thrust from the west; it was the German intention to dominate all Slavic tribes. For many centuries, wars raged between Germany and Poland over the question of Polish sovereignty. Their borders squeezed little by little, Poles found themselves backed up against the Russian empire to the east. It was at that point, in the late eighteenth century, that the Russians and Germans, with the cooperation of Austria-Hungary, decided to slice up Poland, depriving the nation of its independence.

For generations, Poland was partitioned by its neighbors; its people were dominated by the harsh rule of Germany to the west, Austria-Hungary to the south, and Czarist Russia to the east.

Three times the Poles attempted to rid themselves of their powerful tormentors. In 1794 Tadeusz Kosciusko—a trusted military advisor to General George Washington during the American Revolution—led a peasant uprising against the Germans and Russians on both fronts. His struggle was quickly crushed. Three decades later, in 1830, cadets at the Polish Military School in Warsaw, which was governed by the Czarist army, staged an insurrection, but they too were conquered. A third shot at independence took place in 1863, but once again in vain. This time Russia and Germany cracked down. They outlawed the Polish language; thousands of Poles were expelled from their native land and exiled to the desolate plains of Russian Siberia; and Poles were forbidden to own property in the territory occupied by Germany.

During World War I, an underground network known as the Polish Military Organization covertly battled neighbors on all sides for Polish independence. Their efforts were rewarded on January 8, 1918, when President Woodrow Wilson of the United States, in his fourteen conditions for ending the Great War, affirmed Poland's legitimate right to form an independent state. Ten months later, on November 11, Poland officially celebrated its status as an independent country.

But the Poles were not wholly satisfied with the Treaty of Versailles in 1919, which did not concede them the full territory they felt was their due. Under the command of Marshal Jozef Pilsudski, a national hero whose likeness still adorns the mantlepiece of many Polish homes, the Polish army attempted to expand Poland's frontier eastward into Soviet Russia. Initially successful, the Polish army was driven back to Warsaw in the summer of 1920 when Soviet forces launched a major counterattack. The Poles regrouped, and in a determined strategic offensive, chased the Red army back and secured nearly all the land claimed by Poland. In March 1921 the Treaty of Riga, granting Poland new boundaries, was signed, marking the only time the Soviet Union has been decisively defeated at war.

With little help from outside, the Poles rebuilt their ravished nation from the ruins of World War I and 120 years of hostile partitioning. It was a relatively peaceful and enterprising period for Poland, but it was not to last.

On September 1, 1939, Poland was again thrust into crisis when Hitler's Wehrmacht mounted an invasion. Despite guarantees of military protection from Britain and France, Poland stood alone, ravaged unmercifully by the Nazis. On September 17, Soviet troops invaded Poland and occupied much of its eastern territory. The Germans constructed scores of concentration camps inside Poland, at which the Polish death rate—both Jewish and Catholic—numbered in the millions. In the Russian village of Katyn, ten thousand Polish army officers were massacred by Soviet troops.

Despite hopeless odds, Poland did not surrender. Its underground resistance movement, the Home Army (AK), fought long and hard, commanded by General Wladyslaw Sikorski in London, chief of the Polish Government in Exile.

At the Yalta Conference in 1945, United States President Franklin Roosevelt, British Prime Minister Winston Churchill, and Soviet Premier Jozef Stalin drew a line down the middle of Europe, dividing East from West. Poland's fate was sealed. Betrayed by the Western superpowers, Poland was yielded, at the stroke of a pen, to the Soviet sphere of Communist influence.

Communism was not born or cultivated in Poland. It was a system forced upon the Poles by the Soviet Union after World War II. Polish partisans fought Soviet soldiers, mostly in northeast Poland, until the early 1950s.

The Soviet secret police and its Polish equivalent, the UB, gradually rubbed out rebellious remnants of the underground resistance force. The Nazi reign of terror of the Second World War soon became Stalin's reign of terror. Poland was supposed to forget that it had been an independent country before the war. Monuments commemorating Polish independence were routinely knocked down, buried in the ground, and replaced with monuments honoring the Soviet army.

Since the end of World War II and the control of Poland by the Communist Party, the country has been led by six men loyal to Moscow. Wladyslaw Gomulka was the first, in 1945, but he was removed from power in 1948 and sent to jail by his successor, Boleslaw Bierut. But Bierut died suddenly in Moscow seven years later and Gomulka returned to leadership to enjoy fourteen additional years of rule. His final departure was assured after food riots in Gdansk were crushed only by the use of troops. In 1970 Edward Gierek assumed power from Gomulka, but Gierek also was forced to make a quick exit after the strikes and turmoil of 1980 that brought Solidarity and Lech Walesa to worldwide attention. The man chosen to deal with Walesa was Stanislaw Kania, but he lasted only until October 1981, when he was forced to resign and was replaced by General Wojciech Jaruzelski, the first career soldier to be named first secretary of the Communist Party.

The job of leading postwar Poland obviously has not been an easy one for any of the six men, who have had to walk the razor's edge between satisfying the needs and desires of the Polish people and maintaining loyalty to the Kremlin. When revolt erupted within the country, there was always the threat of the Russian Army or the East German military moving into Poland if the leader was unsuccessful in quelling the disturbance. This was the problem that faced Gierek and Kania, and later Jaruzelski, when an obscure worker named Lech Walesa rose from the ranks of Polish labor to threaten directly the Communist government of Warsaw and indirectly Communism throughout Eastern Europe and the Soviet Union.

3.

Lech

Lᴇᴄʜ ᴡᴀʟᴇsᴀ, the man who sought to bring freedom to Poland, was born when his country was in the grip of German occupation. The event occurred in the small rural farming village of Popowo on September 29, 1943, a time when Russian troops were advancing toward Poland in pursuit of a German army defeated at Stalingrad.

The selection of the child's name was an excellent one in view of his later rise to leadership. For centuries Poland was known in the East as Lechistan—Lech's state—a word derived from the mythical founder of the country. Equally fortunate is the meaning of the name Walesa (pronounced Vah-wehn-sah)—it means wanderer, or better still, maverick.

Genealogical records—those in small towns and parishioner archives—were badly kept in Poland, a side effect of unwelcome partitioning and of the country being used as a battlefield in two world wars. It is known that Walesa's paternal great-grandfather was a wealthy farmer with more than two hundred acres of barley, rye, and potato fields to his name. Families in Poland are large, and this farmer was no exception. His land was gradually divided among his descendants into small plots.

Walesa's maternal grandfather, "Grandpa Kaminski," is remembered as an informed, opinionated man and a community leader, while his paternal grandfather is recalled as a man of prudence with a voracious appetite for books and newspapers. Villagers sought the latter's wisdom on political matters as well as on land cultivation and animal breeding. He was twice married and is said to have fathered about twenty children. He secretly belonged to the underground Polish Military Organization.

Lech's father, Boleslaw Walesa, inherited only a small portion of the family farm. The small plot could not provide enough to feed his wife, Feliksa, and their four children—Izabella, Edward, Stanislaw, and the youngest, Lech, or Leszek as he was known. So Boleslaw carved himself a career as a carpenter. He would walk from village to village with his brothers—Jan, Zygmunt, Izydor, Mieczyslaw, Stanislaw, and Aleksander—in search of new projects. They built barns, stables, and small cottages. As one current resident of Popowo remembers, "They were master carpenters; the best in the area."

In 1944, near the end of World War II, the Germans ordered all of Popowo's men to a forced labor camp in Mlyniec for trench digging. Boleslaw ignored the order and was arrested, beaten for his insubordination, and sent off to join the others. Conditions in Mlyniec that winter were abominable. Workers slept with one blanket each in unheated wooden huts at temperatures well below freezing. For Boleslaw the exposure, the constant work, and numerous beatings were fatal. He died within a year of his return home to Popowo in 1945. His youngest son, Lech, was then three years old.

Boleslaw's brother Stanislaw looked after Feliksa and her four children. Eventually they married and Feliksa bore three further sons, Tadeusz, Zygmunt, and Wojciech.

Lech was raised in a tiny concrete cottage in the Kujawy region of central Poland. The cottage today stands empty, a symbol of the social trend in Poland to move from the countryside into cities in search of an easier life. During his boyhood years, Lech would earn pocket money at the local brickyard, carrying the raw, freshly packed bricks to the furnace. He was a generous lad, known to share the sweet cakes he could afford with his playmates. In 1950, at age seven, formal education began in the nearby village of Chalin. The schoolhouse was comprised of three small classrooms and a large wooden porch. Lech was an average student, remembered only for his daring.

"We used to go after school to the lake shore," remembers Pani Lewandowska, a classmate. "Leszek liked to impress us with his courage. He swam a longer distance than any other boy."

At age fifteen, Walesa was enrolled in a boarding trade school located in County Lipno, on the banks of the River Mien. His training was in agricultural mechanics. Walesa enjoyed the practical work and thrived on operating and repairing farm machinery. He liked to work with his hands and was a member of the school's model airplane club. But student number 1488 did not excel in his academic studies. Headmaster Jerzy Rybacki recollects that Walesa's grades were mostly C's and D's, with an occasional B in physical education. He consistently failed a course in history.

The only A Lech ever earned was for conduct, which is surprising, since socially Walesa is remembered as a teenager of brawling rowdiness. His conduct grade was lowered a notch after three reprimands for smoking cigarettes in the dormitory. And that was not his only transgression. The following note can be found in Walesa's school records: "Lech Walesa was caught leaving the dormitory bareheaded, with his school cap in his pocket."

When Walesa emerged in August 1980 as an internationally celebrated strike leader, his former teachers gathered at the old school to discuss their recollections of him. One instructor remembered Walesa as a swash-buckler, a cheerful fellow who could diffuse any discord with a few humorous words. Stanislaw Marciniak, another teacher, recalled that "if someone didn't agree with Lech's opinion he was sore. He'd feel like they did him wrong."

Walesa was remembered best for his bravery. Once, during a discussion on the meaning of courage, a teacher asked his students which of them had the guts to visit the local cemetery at midnight. Only Walesa perked up. "Me!" he exclaimed. And he did, that very night.

Walesa graduated from trade school in 1961 at the age of eighteen. He took a job as a garage mechanic, a specialist in electrical matters, in the village of Locho-cin, not far from his native Popowo. Walesa got along well with his workmates, remembered at the garage for his good humor and easygoing nature. He enjoyed drinking, parties, and girls. A former work mate remembers Walesa as "smart, fast in work, and fast in life."

In his early manhood, Walesa rediscovered the Catholicism he had known during childhood but later neglected. "One day," he remembers, "I felt very cold, very tired, and I started looking for a place to rest. There was nothing around but a church. So I entered the church and sat down on a bench. And I immediately got well."

In 1963 Walesa began his compulsory two-year military service. He served in an artillery unit in the coastal town of Koszalin, was soon promoted to the rank of corporal and commanded his own squad. Faithful to a family tradition, Walesa cultivated a full, bristling moustache. Corporal Walesa was said to exact discipline from his men not by bullying, but by humoring them.

When General Jaruzelski became prime minister in February 1981, one of his first orders was to demand a look at Walesa's military record. There he discovered official reports of Walesa's "enormous leader's instinct." According to his file, Walesa was a "natural-born commander," capable of making "flash decisions."

Walesa declined an invitation to join an officers training program and returned to his job in Lochocin after completing military service. He soon grew restless, though, with his eight-hour-a-day, Monday-to-Saturday routine. One morning he packed his bags, bid his work mates farewell, and set out to make an exciting new life for himself in the city of Gdynia. But en route to his destination, Walesa's train made a station stop in Gdansk. Walesa disembarked in search of a beer to quench his thirst. When he turned around, the train was gone, so Walesa decided to make Gdansk his new home instead of Gdynia. The year was 1967.

Walesa quickly found a job as an electrician at the Lenin Shipyard. His first foreman, Alojzy Mosinski, remembers Walesa as energetic and curious. "He didn't know how to work in a shipyard, but he learned fast."

Henryk Lenarciak, who was to become one of Walesa's closest shipyard friends, recalls Walesa's great passion for chess, which he would skillfully play during lunch breaks.

Walesa himself remembers his early years at the shipyard with great fondness: "No wife, no children— the first girlfriend, then the next . . . and next . . . oh boy!"

But those days as a bachelor were not to last. Walesa soon discovered the young lady with whom he fell in love. They met in the autumn of 1968 in a florist's shop on Swierczewskiego Street where she worked. Lech had stopped in the small shop to buy flowers. It was love at first sight.

Miroslawa Danuta Golos, a slim, attractive girl six years younger than Walesa, had moved from a small village in eastern Poland to join her older sister in Gdansk.

Lech and Miroslawa were married on November 8, 1969. They moved into a tiny apartment, which they shared with another couple. Their first son, Bogdan, was born on October 6 the following year, only two months before the bloody hunger riots that would jolt Gdansk and alter the career of Lech Walesa.

———————

On Saturday, December 12, 1970, the Polish government announced plans to double food prices. Early Monday morning a thousand shipyard workers in

Gdansk gathered outside the shipyard management building. From there they marched to district Party headquarters. Five representatives disappeared inside to submit a written protest of the price increases. They did not come out.

The demonstrators outside the building were enraged. They marched to the local radio station and attempted to seize control and broadcast their grievances. Although they were able to penetrate the building, the workers were thwarted at the last minute by a lone technician, who managed to shut down the station's transmitter.

The workers took to the streets, looting shops and fighting battles with police throughout the long day and night.

At sunrise the next morning, ten thousand protestors —shipyard workers, now joined by the longshoremen —marched to police headquarters and loudly demanded the release of their five imprisoned comrades.

One of the strike leaders, twenty-seven-year-old Walesa, scurried up a telephone booth to address the unruly mob. He tried in vain to persuade the protestors to leave the area peacefully. The frenzied mob attempted to storm police headquarters. Shouts and screams filled the morning air as policemen, hopelessly outnumbered, retaliated with truncheons and tear gas.

In the confusion Walesa sought out Commander Stasiak and pleaded with the police chief not to use guns. Walesa tried again to calm the rampaging crowd. He appeared at an open window inside the police building and called down below to his comrades. He was met with shouts of "Traitor!" Angry workers hurled stones at him, until he threw down his shipyard hardhat in fury. The crowd grew quiet as Walesa alternately argued and reasoned with them for thirty minutes, finally convincing them to back off.

The calm was short-lived. The protestors regrouped and focused their attention on the district Party headquarters a mile away. Molotov cocktails were tossed at the building and the workers cheered as the building became engulfed in flames. It burned to the ground as the rebellion spread throughout the city. By evening six persons had been killed and over three hundred injured. As the sun set, the rioting workers returned to the shipyard and organized an occupational strike. Walesa was elected to the strike committee of W-4, his shipyard division, and appointed to the committee's five-member presidium.

In the early hours of Wednesday morning, army units were ordered into Gdansk. Tanks and armored vehicles stood guard at all the government buildings and outside the shipyard gates. (Soldiers had been told that the German minority of Gdansk had started an "anti-Poland uprising.")

Inside the shipyard, strike leaders could not quell the angry tempers around them. When groups of workers exited the shipyard gates, the soldiers opened fire with automatic rifles. Three workers fell to the ground, dead. A fourth died en route to the hospital.

Stunned silence followed the volley of shots. The incredulous strikers quietly laid out their dead comrades on makeshift stretchers—old wooden doors—and slowly marched into the city, displaying the martyrs. The city folk were enraged with horror. The fighting started up again and continued throughout the afternoon; gunshots and piercing screams echoed up and down Gdansk's narrow winding streets and blood splattered the cobblestones.

That night the authorities declared martial law and threatened to storm the shipyard with troops and tanks. Outmaneuvered and exhausted, the striking workers gave up. The bloody riots were over.

But in neighboring Gdynia the frenzy continued. There is still confusion over a great tragedy that occurred in Gdynia early Thursday morning. One government official had appealed to the shipyard workers to return to work. Another gave police an order to shoot anyone attempting to enter the shipyard. So when laborers appeared for work they were greeted not with appreciation but with bullets. Many workers were killed; hundreds more wounded. (The findings of an official inquiry into the blunder were never publicly disclosed.)

Official figures indicate that forty-five persons were killed in Gdansk and Gdynia, but unofficially the death toll is thought to be three times that.

Three days after the riots ended, Communist Party

First Secretary Wladyslaw Gomulka was toppled by the Party's Central Committee, Poland's highest authority, and replaced with Edward Gierek, first secretary of Poland's Silesian district.

For Walesa, the cause and effect of the riots signaled the start of a long, arduous decade of commitment.

4.

The Agitator

"DECEMBER 1970 was my greatest defeat," Walesa once confessed. "We had a chance, but I was twenty-seven years old and I had no experience. Over ten years I've had a lot of time to rethink everything, to analyze every detail. The spilled blood would not let me forget."

As a strike leader in 1970, Walesa felt guilty and responsible for the workers who were slaughtered. Walesa set out to educate himself. He threw himself into books on psychology and human behavior, spending hours at libraries.

A further result of the 1970 riots was that Walesa was constantly shadowed by officers of the secret police and interrogated, along with the other strike committee members. Henryk Lenarciak, Walesa's close friend and fellow strike leader, recalls how the secret police had attempted to persuade them both to cooperate with the authorities and become informants. "We promptly declined," says Lenarciak, "me in a polite manner, Walesa with fury."

In his new job as first secretary of the Communist Party, Poland's top position, Edward Gierek seemed little affected by the workers' demands. The government's plan to increase food prices was implemented without hesitation.

In mid-January 1971, Gdansk shipyard workers met quietly to formulate a list of demands. One demand called for a major change in the structure and organization of trade unions. Another called for a meeting with Gierek and Prime Minister Piotr Jaroszewicz. Workers waited a week for an answer, but it was not forthcoming. In late January a strike was announced. Its effect was immediate: news arrived from Warsaw that Gierek and Jaroszewicz would meet with representatives of the workers several days later. Walesa and Henryk Lenarciak were elected representatives of their division. Lenarciak, ten years Walesa's senior, did the talking. Walesa listened carefully to the negotiations, diligently noting each promise made by Gierek and Jaroszewicz.

A month later, new local trade union elections were organized. Lenarciak was elected president of the local union and Walesa was selected as the work conditions inspector. "This function suited him most," recalls Lenarciak. "He wanted to understand the mood of the whole shipyard and as a union inspector he had the right to walk anywhere and talk to anybody."

It was a wise position to take. Walesa was able to spread himself out and gain popularity in all corners of the shipyard. Together, Walesa and Lenarciak built up the union's activities, under the watchful eye of the shipyard's management.

In 1972 Walesa withdrew his candidacy for the trade union election. He was bitterly disappointed with the union's lack of authority and, besides, he needed time to organize his own home. His second son, Slawomir, had been born in September and his family had finally been designated a two-room apartment of their own on Wrzosy Street in the outskirts of Gdansk.

On one pretext or another, leaders of the 1970 strike were gradually fired. Walesa, too, was on the Party blacklist. In a private conversation he had muttered, "We shall hang all Reds," and somebody had reported the imprudent remark to a local Party secretary. The shipyard's management soon received an order from the district Party office to fire Walesa. The trade union jumped to Walesa's defense. They saved his job, but the management extracted a pledge from Walesa to keep silent.

It was not to last. At a workers' meeting in February 1976, Walesa lashed out fiercely at Gierek, accusing the first secretary of not keeping promises to the workers accorded years earlier. He also accused Gierek of being a dictator. Shortly thereafter, Walesa was fired from his shipyard job. Walesa's boss tried to intervene and he, too, was fired. The shipyard governors paid Walesa a full month's salary and banished him from the shipyard's grounds.

Walesa appealed to the Labor Commission for the return of his job, but was turned down. Details of Walesa's "troublemaking" activities were whispered to potential employers. Walesa found himself blacklisted.

After months of searching for work, Walesa landed a job as a mechanic at the transport division of Zremb, a construction supplier. Outside work hours he was active in dissident circles and in the underground Free Trade Unions movement.

The Free Trade Unions movement was secretly organized at the end of April 1978 in Gdansk. Its founders were Andrzej Gwiazda, Gwiazda's wife Joanna, and Bogdan Borusewicz.

Borusewicz was a ranking member of KOR, the Workers Defense Committee, an underground group formed immediately after workers' riots in June 1976. These riots, a result of increased food prices, took place in Ursus, outside Warsaw, and Radom, an industrial city. Following the one-day revolt, the government revoked the intended increase, but began to sharply crack down on workers-rights activists. As a result, dissidents from the intelligentsia community, led by Jacek Kuron and Adam Michnik, formed KOR to assist de-

tained workers with legal aid and financial help for
their families. KOR's second role was to spread information throughout Poland of government deception
and illegalities.

"Lech Walesa contacted me in mid-May 1978," recalls Bogdan Borusewicz. "He was an action man. He
had an old van, built with his own hands from spare
parts, and he proposed we use it to organize our secret
meetings."

At the meetings of the Free Trade Unions movement, discussion centered on trade unions, human
rights, workers' rights, contemporary history of Poland
and the country's political situation.

Walesa would walk from one enterprise to the next,
distributing leaflets and underground newspapers. He
became popular in workers' circles and notorious in
police precincts. He was frequently trailed in his travels
by plainclothes officers. The police would even interro-
gate his friends and work mates, advising that they
should steer clear of the troublesome Walesa.

In late 1978 Walesa was appointed to the editorial
board of *Robotnik Wybrzeza* (Coastal Worker), a spin-
off of the popular *Robotnik,* the clandestine newspaper
of the KOR. *Robotnik* had been formed in late 1977 by
a group of intellectuals associated with the KOR. They
included Dariusz Kupiecki and Jan Litynski, both
mathematicians; Helena Luczywo and Irena Woycicka,
economists; Witold Luczywo, an engineer; and Henryk
Wujec, a physicist. The first issue, four typed pages, had

a limited circulation of four hundred copies. (Two years later its circulation would reach twenty thousand.)

Robotnik's operations had to be kept very secret. The police were continually on the lookout for underground newspaper publishers and couriers. The freshly printed edition would be transported in great secrecy from the printer's workshop—usually a secluded house —to another home where copies were packaged in brown paper for distribution in fifty spots throughout Poland. *Robotnik*'s editors were routinely picked up by police, detained for forty-eight hours (the maximum time permitted to hold someone without pressing charges), and sometimes beaten.

Robotnik was by no means Poland's sole underground newspaper. In the late 1970s some sixty different newspapers were distributed throughout the country by underground movements and dissident groups.

Underground book publishing also sprang up as a result of worker unrest. One of the best known such publishers was NOWA, the Independent Publishing House. Its owner, Miroslaw Chojecki, had been arrested forty-four times between 1976 and 1980, and had spent some eight months in prison. Soon after forming his publishing house, Chojecki was fired from the nuclear research institute where he worked as a physicist, beaten by police and dumped in a remote area. His life has been threatened countless times.

NOWA was a mobile operation, always on the run. It published in Polish the works of George Orwell, Alexander Solzhenitsyn, and Günther Grass, all officially censored authors. It also published uncensored accounts of Polish history and government-banned Polish literary works.

At Zremb, where he worked, Walesa was elected to the Self-governing Workers Commission. In late November 1978 Walesa once again lashed out at the economic policies of First Secretary Gierek at an SWC meeting. The workers applauded wildly. Down came an order from management requesting that Walesa be relieved of his job as of December 31. The trade union rallied to Walesa's defense, but Walesa dissuaded the workers from striking because he felt the timing was wrong.

"You have wives and children," explained Walesa. "It's too risky to strike now; we are too weak. But you shouldn't give up hope. Someday we will be more powerful and we shall win."

Privately, Walesa confided to friends that he did not think he would see free trade unions in Poland in his lifetime.

Nineteen seventy-nine was a bad year for Walesa and his family of six. (Two more sons, Przemyslaw and Jaroslaw, were born in 1974 and 1976, respectively. In addition, Miroslaw was pregnant again. Their first daughter, Magdalena, was born in September 1979.) Walesa had no job, no income, and little money. He sold his old van, but it was not enough. Every so often he received a helping hand from the underground, and he worked part time at gas stations when they would have him. The future looked grim.

It was five lean months before Walesa was finally offered a job at Elektromontaz, a large electrical firm. He was still regularly followed and harassed by officers of the secret police.

Meanwhile, Poles throughout the country were becoming increasingly fed up with official propaganda of well-being contrasted by food shortages, inflation, and Party corruption. The idea of free trade unions, unions not controlled by the Party, was gaining credence in all corners of Poland.

In 1977 the Young Poland Movement had begun commemorating each anniversary of the December 1970 riots with a ceremony near the shipyard gates in Gdansk. In 1977, four hundred persons gathered to honor the martyred workers. In 1978 about two thousand persons assembled to remember their comrades. And now, in 1979, the Young Poland Movement wanted Walesa to address the expected crowd. The police routinely detained known strike leaders just before any type of dissident event. But when police came looking for Walesa the day before the ceremony, they were out of luck, having been outwitted by complex safehouse arrangements, which had been specially hatched for the occasion.

Walesa appeared at the ceremony on schedule and addressed an assembly of seven thousand workers. In his emotion-packed speech, Walesa promised that by next year, 1980, a monument will have been built to commemorate the 1970 victims. "If not by government, then every person should bring one stone and we will pile these stones together and build this monument ourselves," he told the crowd.

The crowd thundered its approval.

Once again, Walesa paid for his freedom of speech with his job. Several days before Christmas, Elektromontaz informed Walesa of his impending dismissal.

Broke again, Walesa worked part time wherever he could. He continued to distribute leaflets on a grand scale, even after mass on Sundays, with his whole family in tow, knowing full well that policemen would shy away rather than detain a man surrounded by his children. However, once he was picked up while pushing Magdalena in her baby carriage and stopping to paste leaflets to walls. In this instance, the police dropped baby and carriage off at Walesa's home before continuing the journey to the station house.

Lech and Miroslaw's sixth child, a daughter, Anna, was born the second day of August 1980. One night before the baby was due, police arrived for Walesa. Despite Miroslaw's loud screams, Walesa was led away and detained for the standard forty-eight hours.

Walesa had become famous in his neighborhood for his dissident exploits. There was not a wall in the vicinity free of Walesa's posters and leaflets. Plainclothes police officers were always on hand to monitor his movements. But Walesa kept pushing forward fear-

lessly, refusing to be intimidated by the seemingly un-
beatable force around him. It was only after a woman
named Anna Walentynowicz was dismissed from her
job at the Lenin Shipyard in early August that Walesa
went into hiding at various underground safehouses to
avoid detention.

Walesa's boyhood home

Lech Walesa as a youthful
soldier in the Polish Army

The young Walesa and his bride

Opposite: Early in the Solidarity movement it became apparent that Walesa would be its leader. In one photograph he is applauded by fellow workers and in the other he is carried on their shoulders after successful meetings in August of 1980 with government officials at the Lenin Shipyard in Gdansk.

TYGODNIK

22 maja 1981 roku
Cena 7 zł

8

SŁOWA PRYMASA POLSKI

Podczas mszy świętych, odprawionych na Placu Zamkowym w Warszawie w intencji Papieża w dniu 14 maja, odtworzone zostało z taśm magnetofonowych nastepujace krótkie przemówienie ciężko chorego Księdza Kardynała Prymasa Stefana Wyszyńskiego:

Umiłowani biskupi pomocni, drodzy dziekani, prezbiterzy, Ludu Bożego Kościoła świętego w Ojczyźnie.

Bolesne obarczenia, które wstrząsnęły niedawno całego świata, od chwili gdy złość uległa w głowę Kościoła Chrystusowego, na przyczynia tak wielkich przeniesionych w naszych osobistych doznań i przeżyciach, że uwalniamy ze dzisiaj na niezwykle drobne i chromoto w porównaniu z tym, to dotknęło Ojca Świętego, tym niezmordowanego apostoła i pokoja i miłości w całym świecie. Dotyka to na nawet jakąś bolesną cząstkę jego nieustraszonego apostolstwa...

[...]

STEFAN KARDYNAŁ WYSZYŃSKI
Prymas Polski
Warszawa, Niedziela, 24.05.1981 r.

1. W Tobie, Panie, ufność pokładam, obym nigdy nie był zawstydzony.

2. W sprawiedliwości Twojej ocal i uchroń mnie. Nakłoń ku mnie ucha Twego i wybaw mnie.

3. Bądź dla mnie skałą schronienia, obym mógł tam ujść zawsze. Postanowiłeś mnie ratować, bo Ty jesteś opiekun mój, dla Ciebie moja pieśń pochwalna zawsze.

4. Boże mój, uchroń mnie od ręki nieprawego, od garści krzywdziciela i gwałtownika.

5. Bo Ty jesteś oczekiwaniem moim Panie, nadzieją moją od młodości.

6. Na Tobie polegałem od powicia, od łona matki mojej jesteś opiekun mój, dla Ciebie moja pieśń pochwalne zawsze.

7. Dziwowiskiem stałem się dla wielu, ale to Tobie moja mocna obrona.

8. Pełne były Twojej chwały moje usta, wspaniałości Twojej przez cały dzień.

9. Nie porzucaj mnie w czas mojej starości. Kiedy moje siły ustają, nie opuszczaj mnie.

10. Bo mówią o mnie moi wrogowie, godzący na moje życie weszli w zmowę.

11. I powiadają: „Bóg opuścił go, ścigajcie i pojmajcie, bo nie ma kto by ocalił".

12. Boże, nie stój daleko ode mnie. Boże mój, śpiesz mi na pomoc.

13. Niech będą zawstydzeni i zginą prześladowcy duszy mojej, niech okryją się hańbą i niesławą szukający mojej zguby.

14. Ale ja zawsze zachowam nadzieję i będę dalej pomnażał Twoją chwałę.

15. Usta moje będą opowiadać sprawiedliwość Twoją, przez cały dzień dobrodziejstwa Twoje, a nie znam ich liczby.

16. Pójdę powiadając wszechmoc Boga, Panią, pomny będę jedynie na Twoją sprawiedliwość.

17. Boże, nauczałeś mnie od młodości mojej, i aż do dziś oznajmiam cuda Twoje.

18. Także w starości i wieku sędziwym nie opuszczaj mnie, Boże, aż oznajmię siłę Twojej ręki przyszłemu pokoleniu, każdemu z potomnych wszechmoc Twoją.

19. I sprawiedliwość Twoją, Boże, jak niebo wysoka, Któryś uczynił rzeczy wielkie, Boże, któż równy Tobie?

20. Który dałeś mi doświadczyć utrapień wielu i nieszczęść, i znowu ożywiasz mnie i podnosisz z otchłani ziemskiej.

21. Pomnożysz jeszcze dostojeństwo moje i obracając się ku mnie pocieszysz mnie.

22. I ja też wysławiać będę Ciebie na harfie za wierność Twoją, Boże. Śpiewać będę Tobie grając na cytrze, Święty Izraela.

23. Rozradują się moje wargi, kiedy śpiewać Tobie będę, i dusza moja, którą wyswobodził.

24. I język mój cały dzień głosić opowiadać będzie sprawiedliwość Twoją, bo wstydem będą okryci i hańbą szukający mojej zguby.

KSIĘGA PSALMÓW, PSALM 71
tłumaczył z hebrajskiego CZESŁAW MIŁOSZ

PO ZAMACHU NA PAPIEŻA

OŚWIADCZENIE DELEGACJI „SOLIDARNOŚCI" PRZEBYWAJĄCEJ W JAPONII

Delegacja „Solidarności" z Lechem Wałęsą na czele, przebywająca w Japonii dowiedziała się w godzinach wieczornych tutejszego czasu o zamachu na życie Ojca Świętego Jana Pawła II.

Jesteśmy wstrząśnięci tą wiadomością. Wszystkie nasze uczucia, myśli i modlitwy są w tej chwili przy Ojcu Świętym. Papież Jan Paweł II, głowa Kościoła, jest naszym wielkim rodakiem, naszym honorem i dumą. Był i nami zawsze w naszych najcięższych chwilach i my w tej chwili jesteśmy z Nim. Nie ma dla nas ważniejszej sprawy niż Jego zdrowie i życie.

Łączymy się także z cierpieniem innych ludzi, które stały się ofiarą tego tragicznego wydarzenia. Dzień jutrzejszy dedykujemy naszą modlitwie od naglącej modlitwy o zachowanie życia i utrzesza papieża. Dalsze nasze kroki uzależniamy od wiadomości z Rzymu. Zwracamy się do prasy i środków masowego przekazu, które rejestrują naszą wizytę o zaprezentowanie naszego żalu i skupienia.

Kyoto, 13/14 maja 1981 r.

TELEGRAM KRAJOWEJ KOMISJI POROZUMIEWAWCZEJ

Ojcze Święty
Jesteśmy wstrząśnięci bolesną wiadomością o zamachu na Twoje życie. Twoje cierpienie jest symbolem prawdziwej miłości dla człowieka. W Bogu pokładamy nadzieję na Twój szybki powrót do zdrowia.

Za Krajową Komisję Porozumiewawczą
i MKZ NSZZ „Solidarność" Gdańsk
Bogdan Lis

Gdańsk, 13 V 1981 r.

Z INNYCH TELEGRAMÓW I OŚWIADCZEŃ

Wstrząśnięci wiadomością o zamachu na życie Papieża, zwracamy się z apelem do całego społeczeństwa o nawiązanie wszelkiej działalności rozrywkowej.

Prezydium NSZZ „Solidarność"
Region Mazowsze

Warszawa, dnia 13 V 1981 r.

Wraz z wzburzeniem tragicznym wydarzeniem przepełnia nas wszystkich trwogą i głęboka troska o przyszłość naszej cywilizacji. Dotknęło nas najboleśniej, jak to uczcie można wyobrazić. Łączymy się z milionami naszych rodaków w jednym pragnieniu: jak najszybszego powrotu Ojca Świętego do zdrowia. I oby nigdy więcej w przyszłości taka tragedia się nie wydarzyła.

NSZZ „Solidarność"
Region Elbląg

Łącząc się z cierpieniem z Ojcem Świętym oraz z wszystkimi ludźmi dobrej woli, dajemy wyraz dezaprobaty dla terroru, przemocy i gwałtu jakie ujawniają się coraz silniej w życiu codziennym...

Stoimy na stanowisku przeświadczeni, szacunku do ludzi i woli powszechnej sprawiedliwości społecznej, wzywamy wszystkie organizacje do niewykonywania powstrzymywania się próbom gwałtu i przemocy, narodem Ojczyzny i na całym świecie.

NSZZ „Solidarność"
ZWCh Chemitex Wistom
w Tomaszowie Maz.

Jak wielka była dusza Polaków, gdy przedstawiciel narodu naszego dostąpił najwyższych zaszczytów Kościoła katolickiego, tak jesteśmy większej jak w chwili obecnej nasz ból, płacz i przygnębienie...

NSZZ „Solidarność"
we Włoszczowie

Strzelając do Ciebie, strzelano do samotnych i do sierot, do ludzi uwierzających, którzy oddali życie za Twoje życie. Modlimy się także za tych, którzy z bronią w ręku czyhają na innych, modlimy się także za tych, którzy dziś strzelali do Ciebie. Wybaczamy im tak jak Ty wybaczasz Całym jestem o duszą będziemy za nimi w tej ciężkiej chwili z naszego świata. Po to jest nasz Tydzień. Po to jest solidarność, Solidarność nasza z wszystkimi ludźmi dobrej woli.

MKZ NSZZ „Solidarność"
Regionu Świętokrzyskiego

DOKOŃCZENIE NA STR. 2

Listy
dziś na stronie 16

As Solidarity grew in strength it was able to publish its ow

Wszyscy obywatele są obrońcami całości i swobód narodowych

(Konstytucja 3 Maja 1791)

rok I

14

Solidarność

Jastrzębie

Tygodnik Regionu Śląsko – Dąbrowskiego

KATOWICE, 11 SIERPNIA 1981 CENA 8 ZŁ

ZREMB w Tychach, 7 sierpnia, między godz. 6 a 10. Porządek i dyscyplina w czasie strajku stały się już czymś oczywistym. Fot. TADEUSZ KLUBA

OSTRZEGAWCZY

Pierwsza zmiana przychodzi na szóstą tak jak w każdy roboczy dzień. Do pracy przystępują ludzie ze służb utrzymania ruchu — wentylacja, stacja pomp, szyby, stacja ratownicza. Załoga zbiera się w cechowni: 637 górników dołowych, 325 z powierzchni, solidarnie i w komplecie. Wczoraj przeprowadzono wśród załogi coś w rodzaju referendum: pytano kto strajkuje, a kto jest przeciw. Na całą załogę kopalni „Gottwald" licząca 5.300 pracowników od strajku wstrzymało się pięciu, nie licząc dyrekcji i egzekutywy...

Dziś na pierwszej zmianie są w cechowni wszyscy: górnicy dołowi, ludzie z administracji, sortowni, dozór prawie cały. Przed obrazem górniczej patronki utworzył się ludzki krąg, stoją w milczeniu, głos przez megafon mówi:

„Szczęść Boże. W związku z ogłoszonym strajkiem chcę wyjaśnić okoliczności, jakie zmusiły nas do podjęcia tej decyzji. Powodem tego są niezałatwione porozumienia zawarte w Gdańsku i nasze górnicze w Jastrzębiu. Od tego czasu minęło 11 miesięcy, realizacja postulatów zatrzymała się w miejscu. Zaopatrzenie w żywność pogarsza się z dnia na dzień. Obcięto racje żywnościowe naszym rodzinom a więc tym samym i nam górnikom. Nasze rodziny godzinami wystają w kolejkach"

Głos mocny, dobitny. [illegible] **Władysław Pietruszka**, działacz związkowy i partyjny, [illegible]

— Takich jak ja, uczciwych działaczy robotniczych jest na „Gottwaldzie" wielu — [illegible] — Legitymacji nie złożyliśmy, bo przede wszystkim należało rozliczyć tych, którzy zapomnieli o swych obowiązkach wobec załogi i społeczeństwa, a na robotniczej krzywdzie zbili majątki. Rozliczaliśmy Zdzisława Grudnia — członka tutejszej organizacji partyjnej — ale nie do końca. Dlaczego ta człowiek, który wyniósł w siatce z placu kopalnianego kilka kilogramów węgla ma zaraz wyrok 5000 zł grzywny. Znam tę sprawę osobiście. A nasi prominenci, skompromitowani przed narodem, którzy kradli miliony, nadal cieszą się wolnością. Dlaczego nie pozbawiono pana Grudnia mandatu poselskiego, tylko delikatnie oczekiwano aż on sam zechce go złożyć? Kiedy — pytam się — ludzie na stanowiskach będą reprezentować faktyczne autorytet — kompetencje, fachowość, energię, przedsiębiorczość.

[illegible]

„Boże coś Polskę przez tak liczne wieki otaczał blaskiem potęgi i chwały, coś ją osłaniał tarczą swej opieki...!

[illegible] komitet zakładowy PZPR uznaje słuszność postulatów załogi i popiera je. Sprzeciwia się strajkowi.

Rajmund Wczasek [illegible] **Tadeuszem Pietruszką** [illegible] Strajk przebiega zgodnie z planem, akcję przygotowano bardzo starannie. Strajk to konieczność. Nie chcieliśmy żadnej konfrontacji. Dziś na cechowni zapoznaliśmy załogę z projektem samorządu robotniczego. Jest prośba do was, do Zarządu Regionu, potrzebna nam jest lepsza informacja na ten temat, brakuje nam materiałów informacyjnych.

(CIĄG DALSZY NA STR. 6)

OŚWIADCZENIE ZARZĄDU REGIONU ŚLĄSKO-DĄBROWSKIEGO Z 7 VIII 1981

Zarząd Regionu Śląsko-Dąbrowskiego NSZZ „Solidarność" stwierdza, iż dzisiejsza akcja strajkowa w regionie jest protestem przeciw pogłębianiu katastrofy gospodarczej kraju. Władze nie wykorzystują wielkiego społecznego kredytu cierpliwości i nie prowadzą należycie działań potrzebnych dla rzeczywistego odrodzenia Polski. Propozycje reform wysuwane przez najpoważniejszą część specjalistów są odrzucane, zaś środki zaradcze podejmowane przez władze nie zmierzają do zlikwidowania przyczyn kryzysu. Naród nasz jest oburzony nie tylko dlatego, iż zagrożone zostały podstawy normalnej egzystencji, lecz przede wszystkim dlatego, iż nie widzi dróg poprawy przy obecnym systemie gospodarowania krajem. Statutowym celem naszego związku jest ochrona praw pracowniczych poprzez oddziaływanie na kształtowanie polityki gospodarczej i społecznej. Musimy występować zdecydowanie w tej sprawie. Stwierdzamy też, że źródłem największego niebezpieczeństwa dla Polski jest brak istotnych działań dla jej naprawy, nie zaś naciski społeczne zmierzające do rozpoczęcia wreszcie procesu odnowy gospodarczej.

Za Zarząd
Leszek Waliszewski

O ROKU ÓW!

(lipiec'80 – lipiec'81)

Minęło kolejnych, dwanaście miesięcy z życia Polski. Miesięcy niezwykłych, obfitujących w wydarzenia, jakim brak analogii w przeszłości. Miesięcy znaczonych gniewem, nadzieją, zwątpieniem, walką, oczekiwaniem, radością, rozczarowaniem, ale i wiarą w sens tego wszystkiego, co dzieje się za oknami. Oto ich zapis:

LIPIEC '80

● (1) Wprowadzono znaczną podwyżkę cen niektórych gatunków wędlin i mięsa, nie ogłaszając jednak żadnego komunikatu. W sklepach pojawiły się po cenach komercyjnych te gatunki mięsa, które dotychczas sprzedawano po cenach cyukowych (kwalifikowanie niższych) ● Strajk w Fabryce Obrabiarek Specjalizowanych PONAR (Tarnów). ● (2) W Tczewie zastrajkowały I i II zmiana w fabryce części samochodowych POLMO, domagając się podwyżki płac rekompensującej podwyżkę cen mięsa. ● Opublikowano komunikat PAP o przesunięciu niektórych gatunków mięsa i wędlin do sklepów komercyjnych. ● Strajki m.in. w Stoczni Gdańskiej, Hucie Warszawa, Fabryce Lamp Kineskopowych, Żyrardowskich Zakładach Tkanin Technicznych. ● (9) Strajk w WSK Świdnik i Fabryce Samochodów Ciężarowych w Lublinie. ● „W lipcu strajki objęły około 81 tys. osób w 177 zakładach pracy" — informacja za „Nowymi Drogami" nr 10–11 z 1980 r.

SIERPIEŃ '80

● (1–10) Druga fala strajków, która objęła zakłady pracy w Łodzi, Kaliszu, Wrocławiu, Lublinie, Warszawie i szeregu innych miejscowości. Krajowe środki przekazu milczą na ten temat.

● I sekretarz KC PZPR, Edward Gierek, spędza urlop na Krymie.

● (14) Trzecią falę strajkową zainaugurował strajk w Stoczni im. Lenina w Gdańsku. ● Powstaje Międzyzakładowy Komitet Strajkowy z Lechem Wałęsą na czele. MKS formułuje listę 21 postulatów zawierających m.in. żądanie możliwości utworzenia wolnych związków zawodowych. ● (15) E. Gierek wraca z Krymu. Tego samego dnia odbywa się posiedzenie Biura Politycznego. Wieczorem TV transmituje uspokajające przemówienie E. Babiucha ● (18) Telewizyjne przemówienie E. Gierka. ● BP i rząd powołują specjalną komisję do rozpatrzenia postulatów załóg Wybrzeża. Na jej czele staje wicepremier Pyka. Komisja wyjeżdża do Gdańska, nie podejmuje rozmów z MKS. ● Działa również MKS w Szczecinie. Wysuwa listę 36 postulatów podobnych w treści do gdańskich. Do Szczecina udaje się komisja rządowa z wicepremierem Barcikowskim na czele. ● (20) Komunikat PAP — „Nadal sparaliżowane jest życie Trójmia-

(CIĄG DALSZY NA STR. 4)

[ne]wspapers, giving the movement direct links to the Polish people.

Although he became the hero of the Polish people, Walesa maintained his closeness with his wife and children.

Opposite, top: Walesa and his aides, some of them Polish intellectuals, met many times with government negotiators. In this photograph, taken on August 28, 1980, Walesa sits across from government official Mieczyslaw Jagieslski at the Lenin Shipyard.

Opposite, bottom: Walesa is a devout Catholic, and he was given firm support by the Church in his leadership of Solidarity. Here Cardinal Stefan Wyszynski walks with Walesa in November 1980 after the Polish Supreme Court overturned a lower court decision that tried to limit the independence of the union.

Following page: Portrait of a leader

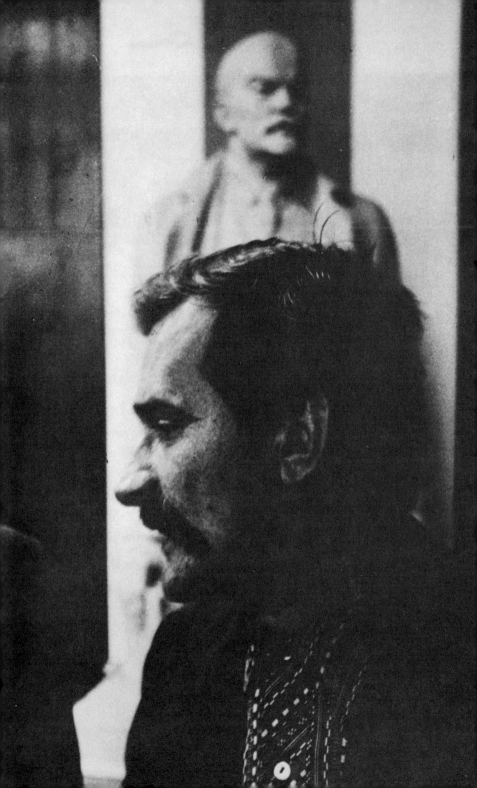

5.

"I Declare a Strike!"

THE SUMMER of 1980 was cold and rainy in Poland; politically, it was the country's hottest summer since the Second World War.

It began with a commonplace decision—an announcement by the government to raise food prices on July first. The following day, July second, thousands of workers throughout Poland put down their tools in protest.

At the Ursus Tractor Factory near Warsaw, scene of the hunger riots in 1976, strikers demanded a pay raise to compensate for the food price hikes, forcing the management to commit itself to a five- to ten-percent wage increase. During the next few days other strikes erupted, spreading sporadically to every corner of Poland. Twenty thousand workers at an aircraft factory in Mielec, in southeast Poland, walked away from their jobs and were quickly promised increased wages. In Warsaw, tram and bus drivers brought their vehicles to a halt, and after several hours had passed their demands for higher pay were met. For the moment, it seemed, the government had control of the situation. But throughout Poland, news of the strikes spread quickly by word of mouth, bypassing the Polish media, which referred only briefly to "short breaks in work." The Poles had learned from past experience to read between the lines of official statements.

By mid-July tension throughout the country increased. Railway workers in the southern city of Lublin called a strike and blockaded the railway tracks with sixty railcars. They were soon followed by Lublin's bus drivers. Finally, all labor activity in the city ground to a halt when eighty thousand workers proclaimed a general strike. Although the Polish media ignored the situation, the strikes could not be hidden. All trains to and from Lublin were canceled and the Polish people knew that there was "something going on."

In Warsaw authorities responded a few days later, sending a special commission to Lublin led by Vice Prime Minister Mieczyslaw Jagielski. An agreement was quickly negotiated, with increased wages offered to the workers. This was followed by an emergency meeting of the Polish Communist Party, which convened in Poland on July 18, and the new pay deals were officially approved. Polish newspapers then reported the labor unrest that had taken place in Lublin, but the message they tried to convey was that the workers need not strike to settle their demands.

A truce was declared but unease remained strong in Lublin. The workers seemed to be waiting for something to happen, perhaps a signal from someone somewhere that Poles throughout the country were ready for a showdown with the government. The signal finally came, in mid-August, from Gdansk, Poland's most important seaport and the scene of bloody food riots in 1970.

Gdansk is the seaside capital of Poland. The old part of town is Gothic medieval, a charming picturesque port on the Baltic Sea made up of narrow, winding streets, ancient churches, and antiquated mills. With neighboring Gdynia and Sopot, it forms a tricity area with a combined population of about 850,000. Gdynia is the modern community, constructed quickly in the late 1930s. Its principal business is shipbuilding. Sopot is the recreational center. It boasts a four-mile beach and a popular wooden pier, which the workers of Gdansk and Gdynia visit whenever possible for sun and relaxation.

When laborers from the Lenin Shipyard, the most important industry in Gdansk, made their way to work on buses and trams on Thursday morning, August 14, they were greeted with copies of *Robotnik* (Worker), the illegal underground newspaper. The paper called on the workers to demand the immediate reinstatement of fifty-one-year-old Anna Walentynowicz. A cofounder of the unlawful Free Trade Unions movement and a widowed mother of two children, Anna was known best by her fellow workers for her annual collection of flowers in memory of the riot victims of 1970. She was ill and had been abruptly fired from her shipyard job as a crane operator several days earlier, only five months before her planned retirement. In taking this action, the shipyard management broke an official social security regulation: No one may be fired during an illness, especially after thirty years employment. The shipyard workers were furious and some were ready to take action.

At the shipyard locker room, a poster announced the workers' demands: the reinstatement of Anna and a pay rise of thirty dollars per month, plus a special inflation bonus. Heated discussions ensued. Radicals from the Young Poland movement tried to agitate the growing crowd while shipyard foremen tried to calm the workers. The young men from the underground movement were more convincing. Even the older workers were ready for action. They remembered all too well the riots of 1970 when forty-five workers were slain by police and army bullets.

Groups of excited workers stormed out of the locker room carrying protest banners that appeared out of nowhere and marched toward the management building. When they arrived it was 8:00 A.M., and the workers, two thousand strong, stood in silence to honor those killed in the 1970 riots. Emotion was at a peak. Workers began to shout their demands in unison: "Anna back to work!" "Monument to the victims of 1970!" "More money!"

The shipyard's director arrived on the scene with a contingent of managers as the crowd of workers grew to over six thousand.

"We will discuss everything!" the director shouted from atop an excavator, the best vantage point from which to address the unhappy crowd. "We will negotiate! But for now, go back to work!"

Behind the excavator, thirty-six-year-old Lech Walesa scaled a twelve-foot fence and approached the director.

"Do you remember me, Mr. Director?" asked Walesa. "I worked here ten years ago. But in 1976 I was fired and couldn't come back to the shipyard. I am unemployed. But I feel like a shipyard worker and I plan to stay." Then, turning to the crowd, he cried, "I declare a strike!"

Walesa was greeted with deafening applause and shouts of approval by the crowd, which demanded the appearance of Anna Walentynowicz. Shortly after 11:00 A.M. the director dispatched his own limousine to fetch Anna.

"I couldn't believe my eyes," Anna later recalled. "There were flowers for me. All eyes were on me. I almost fainted from emotion."

Following Anna's brief appearance, negotiations were convened between a strike committee and the shipyard's board of governors in one of the yard's conference halls. The strikers' four demands were presented: the reinstatement of Anna Walentynowicz *and* Lech Walesa; a monument to the forty-five victims of the 1970 riots; guarantees of no punishment for any of the strike's participants; a wage increase of sixty dollars per month, plus a family bonus similar to those accorded to employees of the militia and the security service.

After several hours of stormy negotiation, the board agreed only to the monument and the no punishment guarantees. The strikers were not satisfied and organized a strike guard: no one was permitted to enter or leave the shipyard without a special pass. A total alcohol prohibition was proclaimed for the duration of the strike; any vodka discovered was emptied into a sewer. Strikers spent the night of the fourteenth sleeping in offices, the locker room, under trees—anywhere and everywhere.

Early Friday morning the bus and tram drivers of Gdansk joined the strike, as did the shipyard workers in Gdynia. At noon precisely all telephone and telex communication between Gdansk, Gdynia, and the rest of Poland was blocked.

Polish newspapers published brief accounts of the strike, buried on inside pages. Curtly they reported: "Breaks of work are noted in some factories. During these breaks, wage and food supply claims were formulated. The municipal transport in Warsaw was interrupted. Breaks in work are noted in Aleksandrow Lodski (in central Poland) and Gdansk." Even though the reports were lacking in substance, the striking workers in Gdansk now knew they were not alone, and this greatly boosted their morale.

At the Lenin Shipyard, Lech Walesa was elected chairman of the strike committee, and the community of Gdansk began gathering outside the shipyard gates. Wives, daughters, and girl friends brought hot food and drink to their striking men inside. Loudspeakers were set up and details of the negotiations were delivered to the crowd by Walesa. His confident voice and charismatic manner were making their first impression on the Polish people. Meanwhile, other leaders were creating large posters, which they pasted on shipyard walls. They proclaimed: "We Want Bread." "Are You With Us? Go On Strike!" "Man Was Born to Live in Freedom."

At noon the next day, Saturday, the directors of the shipyard retreated from their hardline position and agreed to reinstate Lech and Anna. They also agreed to a forty-five-dollar per month wage increase. At exactly 2:17 P.M. Walesa appeared before the crowd to read the strike agreement over the public address system, seeking from the striking workers and townspeople their approval.

"Do you understand?" demanded Walesa. "Signal me with your applause."

There was a burst of applause.

"Are you sure," continued Walesa, "that no one will hold a grudge against me if I declare this strike over? Do you read me? Should I end the strike?"

There was loud applause.

"Fellows, your delegates and strike committee agree that we have everything we want," declared Walesa. "Our basic demands have been met. This is a good time to end our struggle."

But the struggle had only begun. Unhappy delegates from the Gdynia shipyards, from the railways, from the bus drivers cornered the Lenin Shipyard strike committee and outlined their predicament: Without the help of the Lenin Shipyard, the largest labor force in Gdansk, they, the smaller strike committees, would be suppressed by the authorities.

At 2:25 P.M. the heated dispute made its way from the conference hall to the shipyard gates. Some Lenin Shipyard workers wanted to go home and recover from their two-day ordeal, but others grasped the meaning of their comrades' argument.

Finally, Walesa grabbed a microphone. "Who would like to strike longer?" he asked loudly with a steady voice.

The crowd answered, "We are ready!"

"Who would like to go home?" Walesa asked.

There was deadly silence.

Walesa drew a deep breath and yelled, "We shall strike!"

Once again the shipyard gates were closed. The strike was still on, this time a sympathy strike—a strike of solidarity. On that Saturday afternoon the spirit of Solidarity was born. And from that spirit, the Solidarity movement emerged fifteen days later.

That night Lech Walesa was elected chairman of the newly created Interenterprise Strike Committee, soon to become the nucleus of the Independent Solidarity Union. Walesa, who three days earlier had been virtually unknown, even inside Poland, would soon become recognized worldwide as the leader and inspiration of ten million Polish workers, a man who would change the course of Polish history. For Poland would never again be the same.

6.

The Twenty-one Demands

DURING THE first hours of the solidarity strike in Gdansk on Saturday, August 16, 1980, there was confusion among many of the striking workers. Some believed the strike had ended; others were aware of the new "sympathy" strike. Shipyard managers had tried to take advantage of this confusion, using speeches, leaflets, and local television in an attempt to convince workers to go home and return to work Monday.

Strike committee delegations from the neighboring towns of Elblag and Tczew arrived by car at the shipyard and were permitted inside only after presenting their written credentials. The summer air was filled with excitement. When information arrived confirming the plan of the Bishop of Gdansk to deliver a special mass at the shipyard for striking workers, morale improved. It signified the full support of the Church in their struggle. But the good news was dampened by widespread rumors of a government plan to crush the rebellion with antiriot squads at 6:00 P.M. Strikers were visibly worried, and visions of the tragic riots of 1970 were in the minds of almost everyone. Would history repeat itself, they asked anxiously of each other?

Lech Walesa drove his battery-powered car, which he jokingly referred to as "my Mercedes," to the shipyard's main gate and faced the concerned crowd.

"Are you ready to defend our cause?" he called through the public address system.

"Yes!" responded the anxious strikers.

"Are you ready to defend our cause to the last drop of blood?" Walesa pushed them.

"Yes!" the crowd responded.

"So we strike!" shouted Walesa hoarsely. "And we must prepare to defend our shipyard!"

As 6:00 P.M. approached, strike guards confiscated film from secret police agents who, disguised as photographers, had been snapping pictures of the strike organizers. The crowd grew scared and nervous. Walesa climbed a wooden ladder erected at the gate to address the troubled men and women. Visibly fatigued, Walesa soothed them with talk about the workers' struggle and "the approaching victory." Although his voice was broken with exhaustion, he began to sing the national anthem, followed by "Boze cos Polske," a traditional religious song. The crowd's fears were quelled. They were ready for anything now.

Six P.M. came and went with no sign of the militia. Inside the conference hall strike committee delegations spent a long night ironing out their differences.

On Sunday morning a priest from St. Brygida Church conducted a mass at the shipyard, followed by a slow procession to the spot where workers were slain by troops in 1970, a few yards outside the gate. A large wooden cross was erected and bunches of flowers were arranged at its base. The crowd of seven thousand stood in hushed silence.

The Interenterprise Strike Committee (ISC) went back to work, their second plenary session. Under the chairmanship of Walesa, representatives from twenty-eight factories formulated their list of demands. It was not until just after midnight that the final list was approved and released.

Excited Western journalists at the shipyard raced for telephones outside the tricity area. Polish journalists could only look on in envy; strict censorship prevented them from mentioning the word *strike,* since strikes are not supposed to exist in a country ruled by representatives of the working class.

The telephone and telex lines between the tricity area and the rest of Poland were still cut off. As a precondition to any negotiation with the authorities, the ISC demanded all communications be restored. Then followed their list of twenty-one demands:

1. Official recognition by the authorities of free trade unions, independent of the Party and employers
2. Guarantee of the right to strike
3. Guarantee of freedom of speech, including legal status for outlawed underground newspapers
4. The reinstatement of the workers fired in the aftermath of the 1970 and 1976 strikes, and all students expelled from the university because of their political activities; and the release of political prisoners
5. Publication and broadcast of news in newspapers, radio, and television about the information of the Interenterprise Strike Committee and its list of demands
6. The authorities to fully inform the public about Poland's socioeconomic status
7. Holiday pay for time spent on strike
8. Salary increase of sixty-six dollars per month
9. Automatic salary increase following increase in prices or currency devaluation
10. Only surplus food to be exported
11. Abolishment of the system under which the best meat is sold in special shops at higher than official prices
12. Introduction of a new management system whereby qualifications are more important than Party membership; the abolishment of special shops open only to police and Party officials

13. Introduction of meat rationing until the meat market is stable
14. A lower retirement age: for men, fifty-five; women, fifty
15. A standard of living increase in the equal pension system
16. Improved work conditions for health service employees
17. Improved standards for kindergardens
18. Three years full pay for maternity leave
19. Shorter waiting periods for apartments
20. Higher expense allowances for workers on a travel assignment
21. Free Saturdays for everyone

The list of demands appealed to almost everyone, blue and white collar workers alike. It appealed to the intelligentsia (the scientific and literary community), the Church, the media, and to the radical underground movements. It was not simply a list of demands, but a political manifesto. Its authors were in awe of what they had done.

The list did *not* appeal to the authorities, who refused to recognize the existence of an interenterprise strike organization and wanted to deal with the strikers only on a local level, factory by factory.

Early Monday morning low-flying aircraft showered the shipyard with thousands of leaflets. "Workers!" the text read. "Don't join the prolonged strike. Think about who this strike suits most"—a reference to the so-called antisocialistic element. Workers read the leaflets with hoots of laughter. Some gathered the leaflets for later use as toilet paper in lavatories.

At 5:50 A.M. the shipyard's management cut off the flow of electricity to the strike committee's public address system. Amid workers' shouts of "Give us back our loudspeakers," the shipyard director appealed in vain, through his own speaker system, for strikers to return to work.

An hour later Walesa arrived at the shipyard gate. He was exhausted, but he looked happy. He led the gathered crowd in a singing of the national anthem and then turned his attention to those outside the gate, workers who had returned home over the weekend and were now waiting anxiously, confused about what their next step should be.

"Don't be afraid," commanded the authoritative Walesa. "We must fight for what rightly belongs to us. Join us, there is no danger. Three cheers for all those who come inside." Their fears only slightly alleviated, the throng slowly, one by one, joined Walesa inside the shipyard gate.

"Three cheers for those who join us!" cried Walesa.

"Hurrah! Hurrah! Hurrah!" the strikers chanted with enthusiasm.

Representatives from other factories and enterprises poured into the shipyard throughout the day. At 9:30 A.M. there were representatives from forty enterprises;

by noon eighty-two enterprises were represented; and by early evening, 156. The entire tricity area—Gdansk, Gdynia, and Sopot—was on strike.

At 8:00 P.M. First Secretary Gierek appeared on Polish television. He had just returned to Warsaw from a holiday on the Black Sea with Soviet Communist Party chief Leonid Brezhnev. Gierek actually used the word *strike* in his broadcast, and he promised wage increases and economic reforms. But he accorded the strikers no political concessions. During his twenty-minute address he stressed that "it is our duty to state that no activity which strikes at the political order of Poland can be tolerated. On this fundamental problem no compromise is possible."

At the shipyard, workers hurled abuse at the image of Gierek on the television screen.

"Does that sonofabitch think we're stupid?" someone yelled.

"The hell with him!" cried another.

Gierek, they felt, was patronizing them with the same old tune.

After Gierek's speech, word reached the shipyard that foundry workers in the university city of Cracow in southern Poland had joined the strike of sympathy. Secret couriers were on their way from Cracow to obtain an authorized list of the ISC's demands.

Out of breath, a messenger arrived at the shipyard gate from Szczecin, a coastal city near the East German border. Szczecin was at a standstill, he announced, its working population on strike.

In Warsaw the authorities began to sweat. They were not accustomed to being confronted by such an organized strike force. Special government commissions were dispatched by air to both Gdansk and Szczecin.

Although Polish television would allow that "life in Gdansk is paralyzed," the Polish media was barred from reporting of strikes elsewhere. Western newsmen, meanwhile, were arriving at the Gdansk shipyard by the busload. The ISC formed a press office to deal with the influx and began to publish the Strike Information Bulletin.

On Tuesday morning the ISC sent a delegation to the district governor. The three delegates were gone only briefly; the governor declined to see them or accept the ISC's list of demands.

That evening the government commission in Gdansk attempted to shatter the new spirit of solidarity by offering individual strike committees pay rises, bonuses, and new housing. By this time 263 enterprises had joined the ISC, and more were on their way. Those who chose to negotiate separately with the government commission soon became exasperated by the commission's refusal to commit itself to a settlement and joined the ISC.

Late Wednesday evening, those tuned in to the BBC's World Service or Voice of America heard John Paul II, the Polish pope, speak for the first time on the unrest inside his homeland.

"We here in Rome," he said, "are united with our fellow Poles whose problems are close to our heart and for which we ask the Lord's aid."

Ecstasy gripped the striking Poles. The Soviet Union, far less pleased, responded by stepping up their efforts to jam the foreign broadcasts.

Another foreign reaction emanated from the International Longshoremen's Association in the United States. Its officials announced it would boycott cargoes to and from Poland as a show of sympathy.

On Thursday, Tadeusz Pyka, head of the government commission in Gdansk, was recalled to Warsaw and replaced by Deputy Premier Mieczyslaw Jagielski. It was Jagielski, a skillful negotiator, who had settled the general strike in Lublin in July.

Jagielski quickly accepted an invitation to negotiate with the ISC, hence recognizing, for the first time, the ISC's authority, which now represented over 350 enterprises.

At a midnight press conference Walesa jubilantly announced that negotiations were scheduled to begin the following day. The news reverberated about the tricity area.

Shortly following Walesa's announcement, two intellectuals from Warsaw arrived at the shipyard gate. They were Tadeusz Mazowiecki, editor of the Catholic monthly magazine *Wiez,* and Dr. Bronislaw Geremek, a historian and organizer of the Flying University, a mobile underground teaching institution. The two had been sent by a group of sixty-four intellectuals who, a day earlier, had signed an open letter to the Polish government appealing for reason and negotiation. The scientific and cultural community had resolved to stand by the striking workers. It was to be the first time that the brains of the country would march arm in arm with the brawn against the government. In 1968 the intellectuals and students had rebelled, but were quickly repressed while the working class remained passive. In both 1970 and 1976 when workers rebelled, it was the intelligentsia's turn to remain indifferent. Now they were united, a force to be reckoned with.

Mazowiecki and Geremek proposed to Walesa the formation of a think tank, experts who would assist the ISC in negotiations with the government. Walesa took the idea to the conference hall where it was quickly approved, unanimously.

At daybreak, Saturday, Walesa ordered that the shipyard be cleaned in anticipation of government guests. Shortly after 2:00 P.M. the district governor, who four days earlier had declined to meet an ISC delegation, arrived at the shipyard to prepare the ground for negotiation. Six hours later the government team, led by Jagielski, reached the shipyard. The strikers watched in breathless silence as the government delegation marched through the gates and into the yard. As the delegates walked toward the meeting hall the workers began to chant, rhythmically, "Le-szek, Le-szek . . . !" Tense excitement was on everyone's face.

The ISC leadership and Jagielski's delegation faced each other for the first time in a small conference room adjoining the meeting hall. There was to be no secrecy; the proceedings were broadcast over the shipyard's loudspeaker system. The talks were tough, Jagielski's smooth eloquence matched against Walesa's provincial earthiness. Jagielski was not prepared for such a well-informed adversary.

The negotiations were suspended after two hours when it became clear that Jagielski could not guarantee a date for the restoration of communications to the tricity area. Jagielski departed for a Central Committee meeting in Warsaw.

In the political shake-up that ensued within the Polish government, six of the Politburo's eleven members were sacked, including Prime Minister Edward Babiuch, two deputy premiers, and Maciej Szczepanski, president of state radio and television.

The striking workers looked on with amusement at the government's disarray. Commented a blunt Walesa, "I've changed six of them; now I'm waiting for the rest."

The Polish media continued to ignore the ISC and its demands, but on Monday, August 25, it finally disclosed the name of the strikers' leader: Lech Walesa. Overnight, Walesa's name became a household word.

That evening, communications between the tricity area and the rest of the country were magically restored, paving the way for serious new negotiation.

Despite a high fever, Walesa led the ISC in negotiation with the government for three hours on Tuesday. For four days the talks continued, Walesa and Jagielski heatedly debating each of the ISC's twenty-one demands. Meanwhile, coal miners in the Silesian region of southern Poland began to strike. Significantly, Silesia had long been recognized as the most Party-loyal part of the country, Edward Gierek's last stronghold and his native territory.

At this point there were strikes in Gdansk, Gdynia, Szczecin, Poznan, Lodz, Wroclaw, Cracow, Kielce, Tarnow, Olsztyn, and the Silesian coal region. Censorship or no, the news was out—and the news was "Strike For Freedom!"

On Sunday, August 31, with virtually no bargaining power, the government surrendered to the ISC. With only a token compromise on one demand (that the future union would be known as the "independent self-governing" trade union instead of "free" trade union), Jagielski, on behalf of the government, signed the twenty-one-point list of demands, point by point. The first independent trade union in a Communist country was established.

At 4:40 P.M. Walesa and Jagielski stood side by side on the stage of the crowded, brightly lit conference hall. On live television, Walesa thanked the deputy premier and then turned to the workers.

"My dear friends," Walesa's voice cracked and his eyes welled with tears, "we shall go back to work on

September first. We fought not only for ourselves, but for the future of our country. We obtained the right to strike, and most of all to form our own independent self-governing trade unions. Our new trade unions will begin tomorrow. I declare this strike over."

Walesa began to sing the national anthem, joined by everyone in the hall. Emotion was at a peak. Even Jagielski had tears in his eyes; it was a patriotic moment for all Poles.

Inside and outside the hall, workers and townspeople literally jumped for joy. The jubilation was not confined to Gdansk. Throughout the country Poles kissed each other on the streets, a celebration comparable only to the conclusion of a war.

In his hand, Walesa waved the final edition of the Strike Information Bulletin which, since August 23, had begun printing the word *Solidarnosc* as its title.

"This news bulletin, *Solidarity,* will be our trade union's magazine," proclaimed Walesa.

Twenty-four hours later the word *Solidarity* would take on a far more important meaning.

7.

Legal Recognition

ON MONDAY, September 1, Walesa arrived at 10:00 A.M. sharp in front of the trade union's new office. It was located at 13 Marchlewskiego Street in the Wrzeszcz quarter of Gdansk. Greeted by about seventy-five well-wishers, Walesa climbed two flights of stairs in the old building and stopped in front of his office door, the well-wishers behind him. He carried a bunch of gladiolas and a wooden crucifix. The office door was locked and there was no sign of a key. Walesa worked on the lock with a key of his own. No luck. Ten minutes later a janitor pushed his way through the crowd and unlocked the door. There were three small rooms, bare of any furnishings except a telephone.

"These are empty rooms," intoned Walesa, "but they

are full of hope." He hung the crucifix on the wall and kissed it. The new independent trade union was open for business.

The first order of the day was a short press conference, Walesa's first as chief of the Gdansk Interenterprise Founding Committee (IFC). Strike committees would be called "founding committees" when no strike was on.

In the afternoon, representatives from enterprises throughout the tricity district met to discuss details of Sunday's agreement and to inform the couriers who had been pouring in from all over the country what messages to take to their founding committee leaders. The new office was too small for the meeting so participants walked to the gymnasium of a nearby school.

During the meeting word arrived by phone that the government had begun releasing political prisoners, dissidents arrested in August and three others who had been arrested earlier in the year.

Representatives from outside the tricity area complained that their local Party leaders were insisting the new agreement applied only to Gdansk and Gdynia. They requested help, a show of solidarity. It was decided then and there by all involved that the name of the new independent trade union in Gdansk would be Solidarity.

Some representatives—they would soon evolve into a radical faction—expressed concern over concessions the ISC had made to the government. These included a promise that the independent trade union would not become a political party, that its leadership would accept the principle of state ownership as a means of production, and that the Communist Party would continue to be recognized as the leading force in Poland.

During the meeting, leaders of the Interenterprise Founding Committee in Wroclaw telephoned. They wanted personal assurances from Walesa, and only Walesa, that the strike in Gdansk was indeed over. Similar calls were taken by Walesa throughout the day.

All across Poland the unions began to organize. Wherever the Party authorities attempted to slow the process, workers rebelled by calling a strike. Silesia was an important example: two hundred thousand striking workers from nineteen coal mines and other enterprises were demanding the same agreement granted to the Baltic towns. They were unaware, because of local Party deception, that they, too, had *already* been officially granted the same new rights.

The confusion was lessened when, on Wednesday, First Secretary Gierek officially informed local Party districts that the new union agreement applied to all.

The following day PAP (the Polish News Agency) announced that the Politburo had appointed a special commission to investigate charges of corruption against Marciej Szczepanski, the former chief of state radio and television. Szczepanski was widely reputed to have enjoyed the confidence of Gierek, at whose home he was warmly and frequently welcomed. Now Szczepanski stood accused of maintaining an opulent life style and misusing public funds. Rumors circulated of Szczepanski's country villas, ever-ready call girls, and foreign bank accounts.

The very next day First Secretary Gierek was ostensibly rushed to hospital with "serious cardiac difficulties." In fact, Gierek had been censured. At a quickly convened Central Committee meeting, he was removed from office and replaced by fifty-three-year-old Stanislaw Kania, a stocky man with a farming background whose Politburo responsibility had been to oversee the army and police. In his inaugural address to the Committee, Kania announced that the new union agreement would be honored by him. "But," he added, "we will have to fight against antisocialist elements because our opponent will try to use this crisis for his own purposes." It was a reference mostly to KOR, the dissident group. Kania did concede that the workers' protest was "not against the principles of socialism, but against the mistakes of the Party."

On Sunday, with the new union one week old, Walesa traveled to Warsaw and was received by Stefan Cardinal Wyszynski, Poland's popular primate. It signaled the Church's approval of the new trade unions.

Strikes flared up again during the second week of September. In Mielec, central Poland, twenty thousand workers at a large aircraft factory called a strike. The local Party secretary in Mielec had told workers they had "no need for independent trade unions" and ordered them all to sign a petition declaring they would not organize one. This sort of local Party recalcitrance summed up the reasons for strikes everywhere—notably in Bialystok, near the Soviet border, and Plock and Tarnow, near the Czech border.

In Warsaw the IFC was designated a small office at 42 Hoza Street as its regional headquarters. Its chairman was Zbigniew Bujak, a twenty-four-year-old electrician from the Ursus Tractor Factory.

Each day thousands of workers climbed the three flights of stairs in the old building to seek young Bujak's advice on setting up independent unions in their own towns and enterprises.

The name Solidarity was not yet known in Warsaw, Wroclaw, and other large cities. Only 50 percent of the workers in the Wroclaw region signed up for membership in the new independent union. Others were confused, intimidated by local Party authorities, and waiting to see what would transpire.

As expected, the government approved administrative procedures for the independent unions. It called for union organizers to register their unions with Warsaw District Court. The court, in turn, would reserve the right to reject applicants deemed hostile to socialist Poland. Organizers could appeal a rejection to the Supreme Court.

"From the moment of registration the trade union becomes a legal body," read the communiqué. "If after registration the union's activity and structure become inconsistent with the law, the Warsaw District Court is permitted to cancel registration."

A meeting of representatives from all Poland's founding committees was convened in Gdansk on September 17 to decide whether they should prepare to register one large union or several regional unions. It took place at the new Gdansk IFC headquarters, the old Hotel Morski on Grunwaldzka Street, a five-floor walk-up.

Walesa welcomed the delegates. "We must work effectively to satisfy everyone," he declared. "We should discuss all our problems and complaints and decide what to do. We must discuss as partners, as equals, for the benefit of all." As he spoke he waved his pipe in the air. (During the shipyard strike Walesa smoked cigarettes incessantly, four packs a day. Now, on doctor's orders, he had switched to a pipe.)

Delegates spoke briefly, each allotted five minutes to explain the condition of each respective founding committee. During the past seventeen days, it was learned, more than three million of the thirteen million workers in Poland had signed up for membership in the new unions; independent trade union committees had been established in approximately thirty-five hundred factories and enterprises. Delegates from southern Poland reported that local Party authorities there were still trying to repel the new unions.

Nearly all the delegates, much to Walesa's dismay, were in favor of a monolithic, united independent union. Walesa tried to dissuade the assembly from such

an approach and proposed a compromise: the formation of a coordinating committee, a central body which
would liaise with the regional independent IFCs and
coordinate union activities. The idea was adopted.

The National Coordination Committee (KKP) of the
Independent Self-governing Trade Union Solidarity, as
it would become known, was established, and Walesa
elected its leader.

Delegates returned to their respective regions with
tape recordings of the proceedings. Copies of the recordings would be used to spread word of the develop-
ment to the rank and file. (No one relied on the Polish
media for union information.)

Walesa and the Gdansk IFC were now advised, on a
regular basis, by a triumvirate brain trust: think tanks
from the Catholic Club (KIK), the intelligentsia, and
the KOR radicals. Together, the three select groups of
advisors prepared a draft program for the Gdansk IFC,
a program that was later to be designated the official
program of Solidarity; in essence, an enlargement of
the twenty-one-point agreement.

"The Independent Self-governing Trade Union,"
read the draft, "represents the interests of the workers
in it, and in their name it negotiates with employers as
well as with administration and the state."

One day after the formation of Solidarity, Walesa
called a press conference and castigated the Party for
"beginning to erode the agreement little by little," add-
ing, "We have been too conciliatory and the authorities

have taken advantage of this." Walesa warned that further strike action could not be ruled out. He was particularly incensed over the Party's handling of a mass which, according to the August agreement, should have been broadcast nationally over the radio. "But now," Walesa reported, "the bishops are asking for our aid because they are being limited to regional transmission and censorship."

The Party backed off. On Sunday, September 21, for the first time since the Second World War, millions of Poles throughout the country tuned in to a live national radio broadcast of a mass from Holy Cross Church in Warsaw. It was a significant occasion. For more than twenty years the Church had pressed for access to the airwaves in order to broadcast mass for invalids and elderly persons who could not otherwise participate. The Party had routinely rejected every appeal.

In his sermon, Bishop Modzelewski emphasized the importance of prayers for truth and freedom and he called for the moral renewal of mankind. "Every Catholic society should have the right to use the mass media," announced the bishop. (A full 90 percent of Poland's thirty-five million population is Roman Catholic.)

Two nights later the express train "Neptune" from Gdansk pulled into Warsaw's Central Railway Station. From it disembarked forty delegates from thirty-four IFCs, led by Solidarity chairman Walesa. They had come to the capital to register their union.

Walesa's contingent was welcomed at the station by Warsaw's IFC leaders and a horde of reporters. They walked the mile to the Grand Hotel where they were booked for the night.

Early the next morning, following religious services at Holy Cross Church, the union delegates assembled at the Catholic Club on Kopernika Street. Together they marched to the Warsaw District Court building, arriving at noon. Walesa had to push his way through the cheering crowd, up the concrete stairs to the second floor. He moved into the packed courtroom and quietly filed the formal application to secure legal status for the Solidarity union. Court officials promised that a review and hearing would be conducted quickly.

Walesa triumphantly emerged from the cold, gray court building with a wide grin and a bunch of red-and-white carnations in his right hand. The crowd outside welcomed him with a standing ovation. "March with us!" the people shouted. So instead of taking his chartered bus to the next stop, the Tomb of the Unknown Soldier, Walesa walked the two miles to the sacred monument on this crisp sunny day and laid a wreath.

Later in the afternoon Walesa and his team met with government leaders, including Deputy Premier Jagielski. After the meeting Walesa appeared before ten thousand Solidarity members at a soccer stadium in Ursus. He worked the crowd with natural expertise, climaxing with the national anthem.

Walesa returned home to Gdansk that night a happy

man, but the mood was not to last. The government was dragging its feet: Wage increases had not yet been implemented and its promise to permit Solidarity access to the media was unfulfilled. Moreover, local Party officials were still obstructing Solidarity organizers.

Walesa announced a one-hour nationwide strike for October 3. The government responded with a television appearance by Deputy Prime Minister Kazimierz Barcikowski, who urged Solidarity to cancel the strike. He admitted there had been some foot dragging over wage increases, but argued it was no excuse for a nationwide strike. Barcikowski also charged Solidarity with violating the August agreement, but stopped short of offering an explanation.

On the first day of October Walesa received a letter from Judge Zdzislaw Koscienlniak of Warsaw's District Court. The judge wanted ten changes in the union's statute before he would issue certification, including a declaration that the union recognize the supreme command of the Communist Party. Deputy Premier Jagielski journeyed to Gdansk for emergency talks with Walesa, but Solidarity's leader was more adamant than ever that the national strike would go on as planned. It was to be a major showdown with the authorities. Nobody could know how it would turn out. It would symbolize whether or not Solidarity had the clout to continue, whether or not it was working. Solidarity organizers and Party officials alike held their breath in anticipation.

At exactly twelve noon on Friday, October 3, union sirens blared throughout the country. In Warsaw, buses pulled to the curb and remained motionless. (A long line of empty buses were parked in front of the Central Committee building as Party officials watched nervously from their office windows.) Trams kept moving in accordance with union instructions so residents would not be inconvenienced, but drivers lit their headlights to express support. At the Ursus Tractor Factory production ground to a halt. At the Huta Warszawa steel mill workers gathered outside the management building with large posters: "Solidarity Today—Bread Tomorrow" and "No Decisions About Us Without Us."

In Poznan, a large industrial city in western Poland, sixty factories joined the strike. In Bielsko-Biala, southern Poland, twenty-five factories ceased production. In Cracow over two hundred enterprises were on strike. The heaviest show of support came from the coastal cities on the Baltic.

Walesa excitedly read through telex reports from regional IFCs and announced, "It's a complete success. We've shown that we know how to start and end a strike. That is what we needed to achieve."

Its muscle flexed, Solidarity's membership rose to over six million in the days following the strike. More important, the strike's success aided the Party's liberals in their own internal struggle against Party hardliners, remnants of Gierek's regime. At a hastily convened Central Committee meeting, First Secretary Kania spoke of errors committed by his predecessors. Known to be a moderate within the Party, Kania accused Gierek's closest associates of wielding excessive power and of displaying arrogance and disdain for both the public and the rest of the Party. Kania perceived the workers' revolt not as a protest against socialism, but against Gierek's violations against Party principles.

Following Kania's highly charged address, the Committee dismissed eight members and two district first secretaries, including Edward Babiuch, the former prime minister whose decision to raise meat prices on July 1 triggered the Gdansk shipyard strike. The Committee dropped two others from its body: Marciej Szczepanski, the former president of state radio and television, and his deputy, Eugeniusz Patyk. Both were formally accused of illegal financial activities, hampering official investigations into their dealings, ignoring Party decisions, and muzzling critics.

On October 9 there was surprising news from Stockholm. Polish poet Czeslaw Milosz had been awarded the Nobel Prize in literature. Milosz was virtually unknown in Poland—except in cultural circles—because his works had been banned. He had emigrated to the United States in 1960, become a naturalized citizen in 1970, and was a professor of Slavic languages at the University of California, Berkeley. Approached by Western reporters, a spokesman for the State Publishing Institute in Warsaw expressed delight at Milosz's award and added that Milosz's poems were included in an anthology of Polish poets published in 1972. He neglected to add that only three such poems were included and that the institute had received an official reprimand for publishing a blacklisted poet.

During mid-October Solidarity's legal experts worked briskly to make the union's statute acceptable to Warsaw District Court. They conferred with court representatives and together made six adjustments. The modified statute was dispatched back to the court for further review.

Another group of Solidarity's attorneys drafted a document dealing with the union's access to the mass media, to be presented to the government. This requested permission for Solidarity to publish its own daily newspaper and to be allotted ten minutes a week of network television programming.

Walesa, meanwhile, set off on a whirlwind tour of southern Poland and received a hero's welcome in eight cities.

The popular Cardinal Wyszynski continued to speak out in favor of Solidarity. "I am with you," he told twenty local union leaders in his private chapel in Warsaw. At a meeting with First Secretary Kania on October 22, Wyszynski stressed his intention, softly, as was his manner, but forcefully, to stand behind Solidarity.

At 10:14 A.M. October 24, in courtroom number 252 of Warsaw District Court, Judge Koscielniak opened the proceedings for Solidarity's registration application. He read aloud the full text of the statute and questioned Solidarity's two attorneys, Jan Olszewski and Wieslaw Chrzanowski.

At 2:45 P.M. the judge announced his intention to register Solidarity. He had more to say, but was cut off by loud applause and was obliged to order a five-minute recess. When he returned to the calm courtroom to continue, the judge imposed two new amendments to the statute: one would acknowledge Party supremacy; the other would curb the union's right to call a strike.

The jubilant mood of the courtroom turned to cold fury.

"It's a violation of the freedom and independence of trade unions," declared Walesa, visibly shaken as he exited the courtroom. "We shall never agree. We have repeated many times that we want to decide on our problems alone."

"We should strike! We should strike!" chanted angry workers outside the courthouse. Walesa composed himself and addressed the crowd. There would be a KKP meeting in Gdansk in three days, Walesa explained. "We do not want to act quickly in anger."

Solidarity's legal advisers believed the judge's action illegal. They argued that the court could rule on the statute, but had no authority to amend it. The attorneys vowed they would appeal to the Supreme Court.

Within the Party, the differences between the liberals and hardliners were becoming greater. The liberals were in favor of Solidarity's reforms; the hardliners strongly against. In early October the newly appointed first secretary of the Silesian district, Andrej Zabinski, had met with veteran Party hardliners from the secret police and militia and laid the framework for their war against Solidarity. He suggested trying to corrupt the new union leaders. "We should give them the best offices, cars and money," Zabinski had said. "We should offer them girls and vodka parties, taxi rides to Warsaw, and compile dossiers on them." Zabinski proposed that the secret police spread nasty rumors about union leaders to divert attention from forming new Solidarity branches. "We should punch them like in boxing," he said, "in every possible time and place." Zabinski also recommended infiltrating Solidarity and sabotaging the movement from within.

Zabinski admitted that during Gierek's ten years as first secretary "some comrades overran their limits" in accumulating personal wealth and living a life of luxury at public expense.

Indeed, corruption in Poland mushroomed in the 1970s under Gierek's rule. Gierek's associates from the Silesian region, his native territory, joined the new first secretary in Warsaw after he toppled Gomulka in 1970. They enjoyed new residences in Warsaw, but it was not enough for them. Many built luxurious country villas in Silesia. Zdzislaw Grudzien, "godfather" of the region, built a two-story luxury home complete with oak paneling, parquet floors, bathroom furnishings imported from Austria, and a basement sauna. Funds for Grudzien's dream house were funneled out of the public treasury, cash that had been allotted for street repairs in Katowice, the Silesian capital.

But by far the most opulent structure to be built in Silesia at public expense was the home of mining industry minister Wlodzimierz Lejczak, which included everything down to the last teaspoon—not to mention a small larchwood bed for his pet dog. This dream house was wholly financed by the budgets of several coal mines.

In October 1980 Gierek's "old guard" was scared, and for good reason. Solidarity was already digging up evidence of their corruption.

But if the Party was facing a split, Solidarity was facing the same problem. On October 25 Solidarity's radicals from KOR circles attempted to seize control of the Gdansk IFC leadership. Disciples of KOR chief Jacek Kuron invited five workers from the Gdansk shipyard to an IFC presidium meeting and demanded that they should have the right to vote alongside the twenty presidium members. The act was clearly out of line; only a plenary session of the IFC could elect presidium members. It was an open challenge to chairman Walesa, who angrily threatened to resign and left the meeting hall with three other presidium members behind him.

Two days later Solidarity's two factions met face-to-face at a KKP meeting in Gdansk. The radicals, led by Anna Walentynowicz, pressed Walesa for a general strike in protest over the district court's imposed amendments to Solidarity's statute. Walesa, opposed to such drastic action at this stage, argued in favor of appealing to the Supreme Court. The two largest IFCs supported Walesa. Moderates feared that a general strike at this time would play into the hands of Party hardliners, who wished a showdown with Solidarity. A decision was reached: The option of a general strike would be kept open, but first Solidarity would appeal to the Supreme Court.

The following day Deputy Premier Jagielski arrived in Gdansk for discussion with the KKP leadership. He reaffirmed the government's intention to honor the August agreement and proposed that Walesa meet Prime Minister Pinkowski three days later in Warsaw.

The meeting took place at the large, drab Council of Ministers building. Solidarity leaders came on strong, provoking the prime minister to an outburst. "I will not have a pistol pointed at my head. I am not afraid of your strike," Pinkowski shouted. But tempers were quelled, since both sides were eager to reach a settlement.

That morning Solidarity attorneys filed a registration appeal with the Supreme Court. Pinkowski promised that the court would make a decision by November 10. In turn, Walesa promised that no strike action would be taken before November 10, but warned that a general strike would be called November 12 if the Supreme Court failed to satisfy the union.

Pinkowski compromised on Solidarity's demand for a daily newspaper by approving a weekly paper. Access to radio and television was to be worked out at a later date and a working group was formed to study the request.

Pinkowski also promised to release Solidarity from import duties on almost a score of badly needed printing machines which had been sitting with the Customs Department since September (the machines had been sent by foreign sympathizers).

As promised, the Supreme Court hearing was scheduled for November 10. Early that morning Solidarity's leadership gathered at the Catholic Club. The mood was tense as delegates chain-smoked and sipped on tea. At ten minutes to nine they boarded two buses and were driven to the courthouse. At exactly nine the union leaders entered the small courtroom, which was too tiny for the throng of reporters, attorneys, and delegates who fought for space. One of the spectators walked in with his young daughter on his shoulders. "She should remember this," he explained to court ushers. Everybody understood.

In the midst of the disorder and excitement, thirty-five Western journalists were summoned to the passport office two miles away. First in line was *Christian Science Monitor* correspondent Eric Bourne. "It's expulsion," Bourne confirmed to the others.

At 1:00 P.M. the courtroom doors opened. The faces of Walesa and his attorneys beamed with pleasure. Judge Witold Formanski had overruled the amendments imposed by the district court. Solidarity was legally registered as an independent trade union. Shouts of joy echoed through the long sterile corridors of the courthouse.

At an afternoon press conference, staged at the Nowotko factory, Walesa declared, "We won the first round. Now we start a second phase—consolidation of our movement. It will be a more difficult phase."

Union leaders, journalists, and well-wishers all proceeded to Warsaw's Grand Theatre, where a completely uncensored show, interspersed with government jokes and patriotic songs, had been arranged.

"This evening we can forget the whole world," grinned Walesa. The performance was climaxed with an emotional group-singing of Solidarity's unofficial national anthem, "Let Poland Be Poland."

8.

Man with a Pipe

A MASSIVE revolt of ten million workers is a condition that any government, Communist or otherwise, must fear. When that worker revolt is combined with the support of the nation's thinkers and intellectuals, the rebellion becomes particularly grave and threatening. And when the workers and the intellectuals are led by a leader whose magnetism reaches out and grips every man, woman, and child, the insurrection approaches the point where it cannot be halted.

When Lech Walesa mounted the platform in Gdansk and cried out, "I declare a strike!" the three essentials of successful revolt were at hand to threaten the dominance of the Polish Communist Party and, indeed, the power of the Soviet Union to keep Poland under its thumb. In the end, the Communist Party, if it wished to remain in power, had no other choice but to order the Polish Army to impose martial law upon the country.

In Lech Walesa the workers and the intellectuals had found a leader with that odd, indefinable quality known as charisma. With his bushy moustache, ever-present pipe, and unfashionable clothes, Walesa could hardly be viewed as a Hollywood type. Yet, reporters were quick to notice that men, women, and children in all walks of life were eager to reach out to touch him—the slightest touch was sufficient—if only to feel that, by touching, they were now part of the man who was leading Poland to a new beginning. For women who might have to stand in a designated line for hours merely to purchase a loaf of bread because the government was unable to distribute bread to all stores, the link with Walesa gave them the hope that the future would be better.

During the sixteen months prior to the imposition of martial law and his swift arrest, Walesa was everywhere in Poland, spreading his charm and undoubtedly causing deep terror inside the highest levels of the Polish Communist Party. Around the Western world, people were enthralled by his appearance on their television screens and intrigued at the sight of a humble blue-collar worker giving high government officials their comeuppance.

In the United States, of course, a few second-rate

Madison Avenue and media people tried to reduce Walesa to ordinary standards. At least one large American shaving cream company offered him a million dollars to shave his moustache on camera for a television commercial. But Walesa's moustache was not for sale. It was his trademark. And a weekly magazine based in New York singled out Walesa for being among the worst-dressed men in the world. Syndicated columnist Mike Royko's reaction was: "It probably hasn't occurred to *People* magazine that when someone like Walesa gets up in the morning and wonders if this is the day he is going to provoke the Russians into invading his country, he might not give much thought to whether his tie matches his coat. If he thinks about anything around his neck, it might be a rope."

As Solidarity's chairman, Walesa was not concerned with his clothing. He wore Western denim jeans and corduroy waist jackets when arguing a point with Poland's leaders. He loathed ties, sporting them only on rare occasions, such as a visit with the pope or a foreign head of state. "I am a worker and I will dress like a worker," he declared.

Walesa's jacket lapel was seldom without a badge portraying the Black Madonna of Czestochowa, Poland's main religious shrine. When Walesa was blacklisted and unemployed, his family on the verge of undernourishment, Walesa considered thieving food, but turned instead to the Black Madonna in prayer.

Religious faith played an important role in Walesa's

life during the sixteen months of Solidarity's existence. Each day he attended early morning mass and took Holy Communion.

"Religion is my interior peace and my force," he once said.

Walesa's most trusted union advisers came from Church circles, but he took care to preserve a separation of power between Church and union.

As he traveled around Poland, Walesa's favorite dishes were blood sausage, fried liver, and boiled cabbage, which he washed down with cola or beer. He steered clear of vodka and other hard liquor, except on special occasions. His only "vices" were a yen for Dutch pipe tobacco and a weakness for a pretty face. There was seldom time for relaxation, to play with his six children (a seventh was born during his detention), or to enjoy an hour or two picking mushrooms in the forests, a national Polish pastime.

Before the revolt of the workers, Walesa and his family lived in a cramped two-room apartment. Following his election as leader of Solidarity, he was offered a villa in the country, a splendid new apartment, and a chauffeured car. Walesa rejected the villa, but did accept for his wife and children a six-room apartment at 17D Pilotow Street in Gdansk. As a leader much in demand throughout Poland, he also permitted other people to drive him from one destination to another.

The central point of Walesa's family life was the large wooden table in his kitchen. Family and friends gathered around it to eat and exchange jokes and small talk. Despite a notice on his door that read "Private Home —Please Go To My Office," Walesa was visited by an endless stream of strangers in search of advice. He was awakened late one night by a woman who felt she had been unfairly fired from her job. She had traveled many hours by train with her child to seek Walesa's personal guidance and sympathy. Another night, a drunken male appeared complaining of marital difficulties.

Miroslaw Walesa, known by the diminutive Danusia, stopped working soon after her marriage to care full-time for the children. "She is a marvelous woman, excellent wife, and mother," says Lech. "A bigger hero than me."

The Walesas' eldest son, Bogdan, attempted at age eleven to organize a school strike and have the headmaster replaced. His famous father was obliged to visit the school and apologize.

As Solidarity's leader, Walesa was surrounded by a loyal team of dedicated associates. The union provided him with two pretty secretaries, Anna Kowalczyk, a briskly efficient organizer, and Bozena Rybicka, a young woman with long dark hair, warm eyes, and an ability to ease tension with her charm. Both worked in a room adjoining Walesa's modest studio on the fifth floor of Solidarity's national headquarters on Grunwaldzke Street in Gdansk. Walesa shared his studio with a personal assistant, Andrzej Celinski, the young secretary of the union's KKP presidium. Walesa was accompanied everywhere by a fatherly bodyguard known only as Henryk, a man over sixty with hands the size of small hams. Powerfully built Henryk even slept at the union leader's home.

Walesa's average working day began at 7:00 A.M. Following mass and a breakfast of hot oatmeal, a secretary would brief Walesa on news events in Poland. Between nine and eleven in the morning he received visitors— representatives of regional union branches or factory organizations. Beginning at 11:00 A.M. Walesa attended meetings, on alternate days, of Solidarity's Gdansk branch and the KKP. At 2:00 P.M. Walesa would return home for lunch, followed by a short nap, his wife insistent on both. Walesa was back at his office by 4:00 P.M. and worked until early evening.

When his schedule called for travel to other parts of Poland, Walesa preferred the beige Polish Fiat 125 supplied by the union over trains or planes. His bodyguard Henryk sat up front with Walesa's chauffeur–man Friday, Mieczyslaw Wachowski, an old friend, while Walesa would rest in the back seat, his head snuggled against a pillow on the lap of one of his secretaries while he listened through a radio earphone to the latest news on Voice of America or Radio Free Europe.

"As a boss he is terrific, but unpredictable," said secretary Bozena in September 1981. "He can be nasty at times," added secretary Anna, "but when relaxed he makes everyone laugh with the latest jokes and gossip."

Walesa claimed to be most inspired by the late

French President Charles de Gaulle. Perhaps it explains the dictatorial manner he affected, which so infuriated the union's radicals. Walesa strongly believed that from time to time it was necessary for him to rule Solidarity with an iron fist. This attitude won him many enemies within the union. Walesa justified his heavy-handed style by claiming simply that everything he did was always in the best interest of Solidarity and Poland, take him or leave him.

During his first year as a union leader, Walesa's salary was identical to that of a shipyard worker. It was later raised to twice that amount. He has been awarded many cash prizes (all handed over to the union)—from Sweden and Greece to Philadelphia, which bestowed its Freedom Medal, the city's highest honor. In 1981 Walesa was a chief contender for the Nobel Peace Prize and perhaps someday he may gain that honor.

Early in 1981 Walesa journeyed to Rome and was granted a private audience with a fellow Pole, Pope John Paul II.

Throughout 1981 Walesa was constantly called upon to meet with government officials as Solidarity gained power and the Communist Party's strength diminished. In March Walesa met with Stanislaw Ciosek, minister of trade union affairs, and Vice Premier Mieczyslaw Rakowski. To the right of Walesa is Andrzej Celinski of Solidarity.

Walesa addressing workers at the Ursus Tractor Factory in Warsaw during a nationwide "warning strike"

By the fall of 1981 Solidarity leaders were feeling some security and they met in Gdansk, birthplace of the union, in September. However, Polish and Soviet communist officials were growing increasingly nervous over Solidarity's power, and on September 24 Prime Minister Jaruzelski cautioned the union to moderate its policies and warned that the Army would help the police curb "antistate and anti-Soviet excesses."

Walesa on his thirty-ninth birthday at the Solidarity conference in Gdansk

In October Walesa held high a bouquet of flowers and the bag used to collect the votes after his close election as leader of Solidarity.

In early December police assaulted a student building in Warsaw and Walesa hurried to the scene to address an angry crowd and maintain order.

As Christmas 1981 approached, the end was near for Solidarity. The spirit of the Poles is illustrated by this picture taken outside the Lenin Shipyard in Gdansk. The banner reads: "A people's tribunal is the guarantee for the punishment of the murderers and thieves [Polish government and communist officials] of the Polish people."

9.

Realism and Confrontation

WHEN Solidarity was granted legal registration on November 10, 1980, it appeared that a new relationship had been established between the union's leadership and the government. There was the suggestion that accommodation between the two sides was now in order as compromises were worked out between the demands of the workers and the requirements of the Communist Party. Indeed, four days after the legal benefaction, Walesa and First Secretary Kania met for the first time. The meeting had been organized by liberals within the Communist Party. Walesa and Kania had both been wary of such an encounter; it had taken much persuasion and secret preparation by their advisers to bring them face to face.

The ninety-minute meeting took place in Kania's office at the Central Committee building in Warsaw. "They sniffed at each other like dogs," recalls one of the intermediaries. But they took to each other. Both had grown up in similar, working-class circumstances. There was a mutual sympathy for each other's aims and problems.

"I was surprised," Walesa told his advisers, "by the sincerity of the first secretary." But within a year the "sympathetic" Kania would be ousted from his job.

Between the granting of legal recognition and the departure of Kania, both Walesa and Kania had difficult problems with their advisers and lieutenants. Walesa had to contend with mounting opposition inside Solidarity. The workers were impatient and many were radical. They had waited a long time for social change and now they wanted overnight the new benefits granted them. Walesa's moderate advisers knew that guarantees of higher pay and better living conditions could not be fulfilled immediately.

In the long run, the other Solidarity leaders, including the intellectuals, realized that their union could not exist without Walesa. There was no other leader with his charisma, his ability to talk with government bigwigs, and his God-given knack of reaching out to the Polish people. If some of his associates accused him at this time (and would continue to do so until the imposition of martial law) of being autocratic, Walesa's supporters knew that he was indispensable. And Walesa himself realized that his methods were the only way if Solidarity was to have a chance of survival. Said Walesa of his Solidarity critics in a speech some months later, "I'm afraid there are too many theoreticians among us and not enough realists. We must find our place in the Polish situation of today."

As for the Polish media, it still could not be trusted; it remained under the control of Communist Party hardliners who censored Solidarity's developments. Despite the apparently cordial meeting between Walesa and Kania, the hardliners were displeased with the notion of mutual sympathy between the government and Solidarity. They were determined to undermine Solidarity's progress.

Late in the afternoon of November 20, a squad of uniformed police officers, led by a deputy prosecutor, raided Solidarity's Warsaw office. They searched the premises and uncovered a document that had been leaked to Solidarity. The fourteen-page directive, titled "Notes on Rules of Prosecuting Persons Engaged in Antisocialist Activities," had been composed by Prosecutor-General Lucjan Czubinski, a known hardliner, and dispatched to every prosecutor in Poland. The document sought to depict Solidarity as a product of opposition movements dedicated to the overthrow of the government.

The prosecutor-general's tactic did not surprise Solidarity activists. It was widely known that Czubinski was partly responsible for the so-called "health alleys," long gauntlets of policemen through which workers were forced to run during the riots of 1976. Workers well remembered "health alleys"—and Czubinski.

The document had been leaked to Solidarity printer Jan Narozniak by a young law clerk in the prosecutor's office. Narozniak was not arrested by the raiding party, but was ordered to report the next day to the Ministry of Interior Affairs for a hearing.

When Narozniak failed to return from the ministry, Warsaw Solidarity leader Zbigniew Bujak ordered an immediate printing of the document (a duplicate had been secreted away), along with details of what had occurred at the Warsaw office. Within twenty-four hours every Solidarity branch in the Warsaw region received a copy.

News soon arrived that the law clerk who had leaked the document, Piotr Sapelo, was also arrested. Solidarity's Warsaw branch threatened to call a strike if the two men were not released. At noon on November 24 workers at the Ursus Tractor Factory put down their tools. The strike was on. Many other Warsaw region factories either joined the strike or called a strike alert. Posters affixed to Warsaw buses read: "Today Narozniak, Tomorrow Walesa, Day After Tomorrow YOU!"

Union delegates from throughout Warsaw gathered at the Ursus factory's Culture Club on November 26. The assembly burst into wild applause when one speaker exclaimed, "It's better to die on our feet than live on our knees!" (The next day this slogan would appear on buses and walls throughout the capital.)

The militant mood rose a notch when Bujak reported that talks to settle the conflict had broken down. A spokesman for Warsaw's public transportation announced his workers would strike if the two men were not released by noon the following day. Others promised similar action, including representatives from the Huta Warszawa steel mill. A brief message arrived from Gdansk: The KKP approved Warsaw's strike action and offered its support.

Again, Solidarity and the government looked each other in the eye. Again, the government blinked. A compromise was reached, proposed by Stefan Bratkowski, a liberal Party member and president of the Polish Journalist Association: Narozniak and Sapelo would be released, and Bratkowski would provide a personal guarantee that the two men would not again break the law.

Both men were driven to the Ursus factory where delegates awaited their arrival. Cheers filled the cold night air as they were set free.

December began quietly enough, save the uproar of the Western media. "The Russians are coming!" was a familiar theme, to be used over and over again. Throughout Solidarity's founding and organization, the Western media had entertained a morbid preoccupation with the Soviet Union's role in Poland's internal strife. It was as if newsmen had been trained to look at events in Poland through Soviet-tinted spectacles. They continually speculated over *when* a Soviet invasion force would cross the frontier, rather than *if* such an invasion would ever take place.

On December 4 leaders of the seven Warsaw Pact countries met in Moscow. In a joint statement afterward, the leaders announced they were convinced Poland would overcome its difficulties by itself. This put an end, at least temporarily, to the ghoulish media border watches.

A day later Solidarity's KKP appealed for national peace and reconciliation. It condemned "irresponsible strikes" and assured the workers that the government was sincere. In the streets, Poles were preoccupied with the coming of Christmas—shopping for Christmas trees and ornaments, gifts, and the traditional Christmas feast: borscht, carp, and dumplings.

The ceremony to commemorate the tenth anniversary of the Gdansk hunger riots was one of the most awesome events ever to take place in Eastern Europe. The affair began on December 14 with the arrival of several thousand persons—representatives from Solidarity, the Church, the government, and even the Party. At St. Brygida Church the city orchestra and choir performed Mozart's *Requiem*.

Within two days three hundred thousand persons flooded into Gdansk by train, bus, car, and chartered aircraft. People continued to pour in from every corner of the country—from miners in their black-and-gold dress uniforms to mountain people in their traditional folk dress.

At 4:50 in the afternoon on December 16, an hour after the early winter nightfall, bright floodlights were switched on and bathed in light the new monument dedicated to the workers who died in the 1970 riots. The 140-foot-high steel structure, three crosses, each crowned with an anchor, was the center of attention. The top-quality stainless steel, 134 tons, had been a gift from three Polish steel mills. The three anchors had been crafted at the shipyard. At the base of the monument would flicker an eternal gas flame.

The cross symbolized sacrifice; the anchor, hope; and the eternal flame, life. Three crosses represented the three workers who were slain at the shipyard gate, the spot at which the monument now stood. A large brass plaque on the structure read simply: "They gave their lives so that others could live in dignity." Said Monument Committee chairman Henryk Lenarciak, "This monument should be a symbol not only of suffering but also of faith, hope, and life. May it also be the symbol of national reconciliation and renewal of life in our country."

The ceremony began. At the monument's base stood leaders from Solidarity, the Church, and the government. There was special applause for Cardinal Macharski, personal envoy of Cardinal Wyszynski, who was unwell, and Walesa. The union leader had kept his promise of one year earlier.

At 5:00 P.M. the shipyard sirens cut through the cold damp air. Brass bands played the national anthem.

The names of the twenty-eight riot victims were read aloud, one by one. After each the crowd roared, "He is still among us!" Relatives of the victims climbed the platform to snip a ribbon releasing a forty-foot white-and-red national banner. It ruffled in the wind.

Walesa lit the eternal flame. He faced the huge audience and began his written address, too nervous to speak from memory, his usual custom: "Our country needs internal peace. From this place, in the name of patriotism and peace, I call on all you present here, and upon all Poles, to assume full responsibility for the fate of our Fatherland. I call on you to maintain peace, order, and respect. I call on you for reason and common sense. I call on you to be vigilant in the defense of our security and to maintain the sovereignty of our Fatherland."

Bishop Dabrowski read a telegram from Pope John Paul II: "I am always praying for Poland and its people."

It was an emotional moment.

10.

A False Calm at Christmas

THE MEMORIAL ceremony in Gdansk, and a similar commemoration in nearby Gdynia, gave the impression of harmony between Solidarity and the government. Walesa continued to call for order and emphasized to the nation and to his followers the need for a Christmas truce. But the tranquillity was not to last.

Shortly before the momentous year of 1980 came to a close, the government began to issue ration coupons for meat, the first rationing in Poland since the years immediately following the Second World War. Each person, regardless of age, was rationed 1.1 pounds of choice meat and 1.76 pounds of ham or smoked meat through Christmas until the New Year. The coupons, known as "Polish bucks" because of their green color, did not provide a guarantee of meat; they provided only a guarantee of long lines at the markets. Still, Christmas was happy and peaceful. A midnight mass on Christmas Eve was broadcast live to all of Communist Poland from the chapel at Wawel Castle in Cracow.

The calm was broken just after Christmas with the emergence of two new conflicts. The government requested that only every other Saturday be work free; Solidarity remained adamant that every Saturday be free, as agreed to in August. The second conflict pertained to the legal status of Rural Solidarity, the farmers' union, which had been formed on September 7 in Lisow, a farming village sixty-five miles south of Warsaw. In October Warsaw District Court ruled out registration for Rural Solidarity on the basis that self-employed farmers were not included in the International Labor Organization pact of 1924.

With both conflicts in mind, Solidarity's leadership convened a KKP meeting in Gdansk on January 7. Delegates from Warsaw and Silesia stood firm against any compromise on the free-Saturday issue. The Warsaw branch, under the powerful influence of the radical KOR, had already ordered its members to stay away from work all Saturdays. Ten years earlier, delegates argued, Gierek's regime had promised to gradually institute a five-day working week, pledging to complete the transition in 1980. Now in 1981 the government was again proposing to gradually implement a five-day week.

As Solidarity drafted a new resolution resisting the government's alternate-Saturday work plan, Deputy Premier Jagielski appeared on network television. "In no socialist state," Jagielski told the nation, "are there all free Saturdays that were instituted overnight. In Western countries they were not started overnight. We cannot have all free Saturdays, at least for the next five years." Jagielski expressed his wishes for "understanding and agreement." His pleas were rejected at the KKP meeting in Gdansk.

The final Solidarity draft firmly declared that any government sanctions against workers who stayed at home Saturdays "would lead to confrontation . . . strikes included."

As the KKP meeting drew to a close one day before the controversial first Saturday, Politburo member Stefan Olszowski, a well-known hardliner called "Fatso" in liberal circles, asserted in a radio broadcast that the Polish economy could not withstand a five-day work week. The Party, he cautioned, would oppose "all counterrevolutionary steps of this kind." Commenting on Olszowski's broadcast, Walesa suggested that "if the government can prove to us with figures that the country cannot afford a five-day week we are ready to negotiate."

Approximately 70 percent of Poland's work force defied the government and did not report to work Saturday.

With the union and government again at a stalemate,

Walesa departed, on January 13, for his first trip abroad. He had been invited to Italy, along with his wife and several advisers, by three Italian trade unions. But the main reason for a trek to Rome was for an audience with Pope John Paul II. In Rome Walesa also met his proud stepfather, Stanislaw, whom he had not seen for seven years. They kissed and hugged each other at the airport. Stanislaw had emigrated to the United States in 1973 along with Walesa's mother, who had been struck and killed by a car two years later while running for a bus in Bayonne, New Jersey. (Stanislaw died of a stroke in Jersey City in August 1981, aged sixty-five. His body now lies buried next to that of Walesa's mother in a countryside cemetery near Popowo.)

In Walesa's six-day absence from Poland, the Party hardliners had toughened their position in government. Politburo member Tadeusz Grabski, an active hardliner, accused Solidarity of assuming an improper attitude on the free-Saturday issue and of "irresponsible escalation of social tension." The KKP response from Gdansk was one terse statement: "All Saturdays are free. If there is a government reprisal we shall strike."

When the Labor Payments Ministry ordered factory managers to dock a day's pay from the salary of workers who failed to appear on Saturday, sporadic strikes were called around the country.

Walesa arrived back in Warsaw on Monday, January 19, with customs officials according him VIP treatment.

He came home to strikes, strike alerts, and sit-ins—a frenzy of protest in virtually every corner of the country. Walesa was whisked direct from the airport to a consultation with Prime Minister Pinkowski. Their tough talks, lasting four hours, proved fruitless.

Walesa returned home to Gdansk the following day. At a hastily convened session with KKP members he was criticized for not having conferred with the full union leadership before seeing Pinkowski.

Walesa urged the KKP not to support local strikes called for Thursday, but he was outvoted. Following the meeting, a union delegation, led by Walesa, was flown to Warsaw on a government plane for further talks. Six hours of heated negotiation ensued, after which the two sides were no closer to an agreement.

On Thursday strikes raged throughout Poland. They continued on Friday, bringing Warsaw to a standstill and grounding all Polish domestic air travel. The government remained silent.

From Gdansk, Walesa called on Solidarity members nationwide to stay away from work the following day, Saturday. Eighty percent obeyed. The government promptly requested that negotiation be resumed.

On another front, Walesa hurried to the city of Rzeszow in an effort to resolve the farmers' month-long sit-in over the question of legal status for Rural Solidarity. Walesa pledged the union's full support and vowed he would not leave Rzeszow until the government agreed to new talks on Rural Solidarity.

Within a few days a group of KKP members joined Walesa in Rzeszow and called for a one-hour nationwide warning strike on Tuesday, February 3, pending a government settlement on the free-Saturday and Rural Solidarity disputes.

The government quickly responded. Talks were scheduled for January 30. Walesa, with a delegation of KKP members and farmers' representatives, departed from Rzeszow for Warsaw. He appealed to local strike leaders across the country to halt all unauthorized strikes and allow the Solidarity leadership to assume total control.

Negotiations began on the morning of the thirtieth. Walesa and Pinkowski, with their respective advisers, squared off at each other inside the Council of Ministers building. It was only after twelve hours of bargaining that an agreement was finally attained: The government would recognize, in principle, a five-day week, but union members would work one Saturday per month. A Walesa-like compromise had been reached.

As for Rural Solidarity, the other chief conflict, the government agreed to dispatch a commission to Rzeszow for talks with the farmers.

"It's the greatest success we have achieved," sighed an exhausted Walesa, commenting on the long bargaining session.

But the trouble was not yet over. A strike that had started three days earlier in the city of Bielsko-Biala continued to swell and the whole region was at a standstill. Strikers there were demanding the dismissal of several local officials for alleged corruption. Walesa telephoned the strike leaders and requested that they end the strike. When they would not, he journeyed to Bielsko-Biala and read the list of charges against the local officials, and promptly changed his mind about trying to quash the strike.

"It's time to say 'enough,'" Walesa announced with disgust, refusing to budge from the city until the accused local officials were sacked and replaced. Walesa took command of the strike and dispatched an urgent telegram to the KKP in Gdansk requesting they stand by on alert.

Two days later a government delegation arrived in the city, accompanied by Bishop Dabrowski, Cardinal Wyzsinski's personal envoy, and a team of Solidarity advisers. The negotiations began just after midnight and lasted until 5:00 A.M. Bishop Dabrowski smiled broadly as he read the agreement aloud: Prime Minister Pinkowski would accept the resignations of Bielsko-Biala's district governor and his deputies.

On February 10 there was new trouble over Rural Solidarity's application for registration. The Supreme Court proclaimed a negative verdict, citing no legal basis in the Polish law codes for a farmers' union.

The next day Cardinal Wyzsinski issued a strong statement protesting the court's verdict: "The farmers must be guaranteed security and stability, and their right to free assembly as unions must be recognized."

During these hectic hours, a significant new name arose from the ranks of the Polish government and his decisions later in the year would have an important bearing on the destiny of Lech Walesa. He was General Wojciech Jaruzelski, who had been appointed the country's defense minister in 1968. Quite suddenly he was named Poland's new prime minister, replacing Pinkowski, who resigned apparently over the Bielsko-Biala fiasco. Jaruzelski's first announcement was to call for "ninety days of calm." This brought a quick reaction from Walesa.

"The ultimate response to the appeal for a moratorium," declared Walesa, "will depend on what happens during [Rural Solidarity] negotiations with the government."

Jaruzelski and Walesa met in Warsaw on February 14. Jaruzelski appointed a government commission to negotiate with Walesa and the irate farmers in Rzeszow. It was soon agreed that the Supreme Court's negative verdict would be suspended, pending the proposal of a parliamentary bill that would grant farmers a legal right to unionize.

Meanwhile, another segment of Polish society had arisen to challenge the government. At Lodz University students were demanding the right to organize *their* independent union. Repulsed at first by the authorities, the students organized a rambunctious twenty-eight-day sit-in. The government finally caved in and granted authority for the union. But registration was promised only if the students included in their union statutes a clause upholding the Polish Constitution and a clause requiring a majority vote for strike action.

Thus, under Walesa's leadership, three important parts of Poland's population had achieved union status and wide freedoms from the disciplines of the Communist Party—the workers, the farmers, and the students. But as the snows of a brutal winter began to melt throughout the country, so were tensions beginning to increase between the Warsaw and Moscow governments. The Soviets were growing increasingly unhappy with the state of affairs in their East European satellite, and the Polish Communist Party was aware that it could not continue indefinitely giving in to Walesa and Solidarity before Moscow would show its displeasure more forcefully.

II.

Provocations and
Disagreements

IT IS UNCERTAIN how much displeasure was shown by the Kremlin on March 4, 1981, when the pragmatic Jaruzelski and the colorless Kania were in Moscow for talks on the situation in Poland. But an indefinitely worded joint statement issued after the meeting said: "Polish Communists have the strength to turn the course of events."

In Warsaw, Party hardliner Stefan Olszowski interpreted the statement as a reversal of the government's good intentions toward Solidarity. Olszowski was at the helm of an undercover propaganda campaign being waged against the union by the hardliners. They were responsible for the distribution of a handbill titled "Keep Solidarity Polish," which accused several Solidarity supporters of being Zionists.

Hardliner provocations resulted in wildcat strikes in the cities of Radom and Lodz. However, both conflicts were settled in favor of the strikers during a March 10 meeting between Walesa and Jaruzelski. A few days later the issue of registration for Rural Solidarity cropped up again in the city of Bydgoszcz, 120 miles northwest of Warsaw. The farmers felt parliament was moving too slowly in passing a farmers' union bill. Solidarity's Bydgoszcz branch arranged for the farmers' grievances to be heard at a district council meeting.

On March 17, two days before the council was set to meet, contingents of riot police arrived in the city. Several concerned councillors sought the assurances of Jan Rulewski, Solidarity's Bydgoszcz chairman, that the farmers would present their complaints peacefully.

The meeting began at 10:00 P.M. in the district council building. Solidarity delegates sat tight with the farmers while the district councillors plowed through their agenda, point by point. At 1:45 P.M. the meeting was abruptly adjourned. Solidarity delegates were dumbfounded; they had been completely ignored.

"Good heavens—what's going on?" shouted an incredulous Rulewski. "You promised that we could present our demands!"

Shouts filled the air as most of the 149 councillors hurriedly left the meeting hall. Another forty-five councillors remained behind, disturbed over what had transpired. Professor Romuald Kukulowicz, an adviser to Cardinal Wyszynski who was in the council building and overheard the commotion, asked the deputy district governor to apologize to the Solidarity delegation. But the governor, a hardliner, had plans of his own.

Despite warnings that the council building was being closed and locked, Solidarity delegates and sympathetic councillors remained inside throughout the afternoon to draft a statement of disapproval with the council. The deputy district governor arrived on the scene with uniformed and plainclothes police officers and tried, in vain, to persuade the councillors to leave the building. He asked the councillors to at least move to another room. It was an ominous sign. Some councillors refused to budge for fear of the Solidarity delegation's safety. Tension rose a notch when plainclothes police officers began to photograph the Solidarity delegates.

The district attorney arrived next and ordered everyone to leave the premises. He warned that he would command the police to move them if necessary. Rulewski picked up a telephone and called Walesa in Gdansk, but their conversation was cut off after ten seconds. Rulewski and the union activists stalled for time, gaining fifteen minutes to complete their statement with the councillors. As the two groups began to sign the draft, police moved in and divided them. The councillors protested loudly as uniformed policemen began to drag the union delegates out of the hall. The plainclothes officers joined the fracas armed with brass knuckles. It was a violent scene, the police drawing blood with their punches. The beatings continued outside in the building's dimly lit courtyard.

Covered in blood, Rulewski and the other union delegates made their way back to their office where photographs were taken before Rulewski and two others were rushed to a hospital for emergency treatment.

More evidence of the violent incident was soon uncovered. A tape-cassette machine inside the council building hall had been left on and recorded the screams of the union men as they were beaten. Copies of the photographs and cassette tape were dispatched by messenger to Solidarity branches throughout the country. It signaled the impending breakdown of Prime Minister Jaruzelski's ninety-day moratorium.

Walesa and three top Solidarity leaders had already departed Gdansk by car for Bydgoszcz, unaware of the carnage that had taken place but prepared to find trouble. The Polish News Agency reported only that a security force had removed Solidarity activists who attempted to occupy a government building. The next morning, however, photographs of bloodied union members appeared taped to buses in Warsaw and other large cities. A radio broadcaster in Bydgoszcz, fed up with government censorship, transmitted a live report on the beatings. Shortly thereafter all live newscasts in Poland were terminated.

When Walesa arrived he was horrified to discover

what had happened. It was decided at 4:00 A.M. Friday, March 20, to call a two-hour strike for later that morning in the provinces of Bydgoszcz, Torun, and Szczecin —most of northwest Poland. A statement was issued declaring the attack on union members "a deliberate provocation aimed against the government of Prime Minister Jaruzelski."

As news of the beatings spread in Bydgoszcz, more than two thousand persons gathered outside the local union headquarters overlooking the River Brda. Speaking from a first-floor balcony, a Polish flag fluttering behind him, Walesa condemned the attack.

"Someone's claws are getting too long, but we will trim them," he told the crowd. "What happened here in Bydgoszcz was an attack on the union. We shall respond resolutely, but calmly, prudently, and without fear. Our knees are not trembling."

Following Walesa's brief address, the entire KKP presidium arrived in Bydgoszcz. At exactly 11:00 A.M. factory sirens blared and church bells pealed to signal the start of the two-hour strike. Walesa canceled an official trip to France scheduled to begin Sunday.

The government responded by sending a commission, headed by Deputy Prosecutor-General Jozef Zyto, to Bydgoszcz to conduct an official investigation.

Solidarity's KKP decided that a national strike alert should be called beginning Monday, March 23. At the railway yard conference hall, Walesa cautioned KKP members to prepare for "hard and difficult days." He continued, "No one has the right to beat anyone up. These bandits must relinquish their posts." He ended his speech by rejecting the notion that Solidarity should seek a meeting with the government. "The one who has harmed us should come to us," he said.

In Warsaw, Jaruzelski issued a statement expressing his willingness to reach an agreement. But in Bydgoszcz, speaking inside the local union headquarters Friday evening, Deputy Prosecutor-General Zyto said he believed the brutality at the council building was justified and that further investigation should be conducted by the local prosecutor, the very person who ordered the beatings! Zyto's remarks were met with jeers by those who had gathered outside to hear the proceedings over a public address system.

Late Friday night the KKP presidium formulated a list of ten demands. These included the sacking of the deputy district governor, the district first secretary, and the police commander in Bydgoszcz. In a statement drafted by the KKP, all union members were requested to "act calmly, thoughtfully, and with discipline." The presidium announced it would not leave Bydgoszcz until a government delegation arrived.

That same night it was learned that Jan Rulewski had suffered a concussion. A Rural Solidarity organizer, sixty-eight-year-old Michal Bartoszcze, was in more serious condition. He had been flown to a hospital in Warsaw with a suspected blood clot in his brain.

Early Saturday morning mysterious leaflets discrediting Rulewski appeared on the streets. Signed "True Members of Bydgoszcz Solidarity," the leaflets claimed Rulewski's father collaborated with the German army during World War II and accused Rulewski of having tried to avoid military service. "Now he causes chaos and disturbance," the leaflet read, urging that union members "disassociate themselves from people like him." In fact, Rulewski had years earlier been expelled from a military academy over his political views. The leaflets were regarded as too professionally produced to have originated from the primitive Solidarity printing shops.

At twelve noon Saturday Walesa addressed four thousand Bydgoszcz workers from a balcony at the local union headquarters. He reported a telephone conversation he had had that morning with deputy premier Mieczyslaw Rakowski, the newly appointed union overseer. He said a government commission would arrive in Bydgoszcz Sunday, the following day. Walesa, in turn, would travel to Warsaw with a union delegation for talks there with government officials.

"We want to settle the problem without further conflict," Walesa told the crowd. But, he added, "We will not let ourselves be outwitted by the authorities, and if they try to outwit us once again there will not be enough lampposts on which to hang the perpetrators."

On Sunday Walesa's delegation faced Rakowski's government team at the Council of Ministers building. Rakowski declared that he was not afraid of a nationwide general strike. He accused Solidarity of creating chaos around the country and suggested that the Warsaw Pact military maneuvers, then underway and which should have ended that day, had been extended due to the volatile situation in Poland. The seven-hour meeting was a disaster. Talks were suspended for three days.

Things did not go much better in Bydgoszcz. The government commission had arrived, but was not prepared to negotiate an agreement. Their directive was only to study the conflict.

Walesa's delegation returned to Bydgoszcz on Monday. In his opening speech at a KKP meeting convened that afternoon, Walesa tried to mitigate the radical mood of those in attendance. He announced that the authorities were considering the imposition of martial law. "We must consider all options and prepare the rank and file," Walesa said, calling for a united, coordinated action. He spoke of the division within the government and stressed that Solidarity should assist Jaruzelski with his own struggle against the Party hardliners.

KKP members were convinced that a strike had to be called, but heated discussion ensued over what form the strike should take, and when. Walesa proposed that if negotiations with the government on Wednesday failed to achieve anything, a nationwide warning strike should be called for Friday. If this produced no results, an open-ended general strike should commence the following Tuesday.

Many members did not wish to wait for Wednesday's

negotiations with the government. Walesa dramatically appealed for patience. He argued that a general strike was their ultimate weapon and that it should be used first as leverage and then only as a last resort. Walesa was supported by Solidarity's intellectual advisers, the "eggheads," but most members were unmoved, their militancy increasing by the minute.

"Stop this brainwashing here!" shouted a Silesian union chief. "Our vote was clear—general strike!"

A Solidarity leader from Lodz joined in: "We should not take a step back!"

The union's Bielsko-Biala delegate yelled, "We are not interested in the government's silly game. If they really want to negotiate they should come here now!"

Furious, Walesa grabbed a microphone. "Bloody hell, be reasonable!" he shouted. "Are you crazy? You would like to prevent the chance of agreement? Do you know what a general strike is? Can you even imagine what a general strike is?"

There was a hushed silence, the assembly stunned by Walesa's uncharacteristic rage.

Solidarity advisers reasoned once again with the hot-headed KKP members. They explained the organizational difficulties of a general strike; the time necessary to draw up lists of enterprises excluded from the strike for the well-being of the public (including the Soviet oil pipeline to East Germany; "Don't provoke the bear, for God's sake!" a leader advised).

Walesa reiterated his proposal, stressing that it called

for an immediate general strike if the government imposed martial law on the country.

A vote was taken: Twenty-four voted in favor of Walesa's plan, eighteen against. The Silesian representatives requested a second vote. This time nineteen voted yes, twenty-two no, with one abstention. Walesa's proposal was outvoted.

Walesa stood up, grabbed his jacket, and in a controlled anger hissed, "Thank you KKP for everything. I am leaving." With that, Walesa stalked out of the meeting hall. It was 2:40 A.M. The session was adjourned shortly after Walesa's abrupt departure.

In Warsaw, meanwhile, liberal Party member Stefan Bratkowski, president of the Polish Journalist Association, wrote an "Open Letter to My Comrades—Which Direction Will We Choose?" Bratkowski's significant three-page letter, covertly printed and widely distributed throughout Poland, exposed the aims of the "power hungry" hardliners, ambitions that could lead only, Bratkowski wrote, to a "political cemetery." In his letter Bratkowski called on all Party members, especially the rank and file, to demonstrate loudly which bandwagon they choose, hardliners or moderates, confrontation or compromise.

The hardliners, led by Olszowski, attempted to expel Bratkowski from the Party, but even First Secretary Kania rose to Bratkowski's defense at a Politburo meeting.

When the KKP reconvened its meeting, Walesa was

noticeably absent. A letter soon arrived from him stating he would appear at the meeting only after his proposal was approved. Otherwise, Walesa wrote, he would resign his chairmanship.

A third vote was taken. Walesa's plan was approved, thirty-five votes yes, three no, with three abstentions.

A National Strike Committee was elected; ten persons under Walesa's command. It was also decided that farmers and students should be represented on all local strike committees.

The strike plan prompted a swift reply from First Secretary Kania: "The union's appeal for strikes can only be interpreted as an invitation for self-annihilation." The authorities attempted to intimidate workers by broadcasting scenes of Soviet-Polish military maneuvers on television.

Solidarity leaders returned to Gdansk in the early hours of Wednesday and formed a National Strike Headquarters (NSH). The NSH began to formulate and issue precise strike instructions and listed the enterprises excluded from strike action:

1. Health services
2. Foodshops and foodstuff transport
3. Railways
4. The national electrical energy network
5. Community sanitary services
6. Communication services
7. Oil pipelines

Walesa, meanwhile, led a five-man delegation to Warsaw where talks were convened on Wednesday, as scheduled, with a government team. The delegation was welcomed at the gates of the Council of Ministers building by a supportive crowd of fifteen hundred persons, amid shouts of "Stick to your guns."

The meeting lasted only eighty minutes; a recess was called until the following day. Negotiation was then put off until Saturday; the government required time for internal consultations.

Throughout Poland long food lines formed, the longest yet seen, in preparation for the strikes. Liquor stores were shut tight by the authorities after Solidarity demanded a full prohibition to avoid the possibility of drink-induced provocation.

Against a background of "indefinitely extended" Warsaw Pact maneuvers, dwindling national food supplies, and acute anxiety throughout Eastern Europe, the four-hour nationwide warning strike began at 8:00 A.M. on Friday. Signaled by blaring factory sirens, millions of workers throughout Poland put down their tools.

Walesa toured factories in the Warsaw region during the strike. Addressing strikers, he repeatedly denied hardliner charges that Solidarity was an antisocialist or counterrevolutionary force, saying of the hardliners in government, "We will smoke them out like rats."

Over ten million workers participated in the strike. Despite its success, negotiation with the government on Saturday resolved nothing.

Walesa and his delegation met next, for ninety minutes, with Cardinal Wyszynski and Stefan Bratkowski, an intermediary for First Secretary Kania. The cardinal called for moderation, requesting the union give the government more time to meet its demands. His words were not lost on Walesa, who listened quietly, as was his custom when in the cardinal's presence.

Rank-and-file Party members, meanwhile, had responded to Bratkowski's open letter by flooding the Central Committee with resolutions condemning the use of force in Bydgoszcz.

On Sunday a Central Committee plenary session was convened in Warsaw. Deputy Premier Barcikowski began the proceedings with an attack on Solidarity. The union, he charged, was penetrated by persons whose goal it was to create a political organization. Other speakers, however, soon turned the tables, concentrating less on Solidarity and more on distrust inside the Party. The debate grew stormy; three Politburo members, hardliners, threatened to resign. The Committee concluded its meeting by directing that the government be given a free hand to negotiate with Solidarity. Party hardliners were incensed.

On Monday a new round of talks was convened between the union delegation and government officials. The negotiations were tough. Deputy Premier Rakowski declared that the main task before them was to reach a compromise and avert Tuesday's scheduled general strike. Walesa stressed the impor-

tance of registration for Rural Solidarity.
Replied Rakowski, "It is not the most important problem."
Countered Walesa, "Without a solution to the farmers' demands our talks are senseless."
Returned Rakowski, "The most important matter is calling off the strike. Discussion on other matters will lead to no results today."
Answered Walesa, "We could call off the strike right now . . . if our demands are met."
Negotiations were resumed after a short break. Solidarity leaders demanded the dismissal of Deputy Premier Stanislaw Mach, who had been on hand at the district council building in Bydgoszcz just before the beatings had taken place. Rakowski opposed the demand, offering to compromise by dismissing two local Bydgoszcz officials. The union men were dissatisfied; they wanted Mach's head. Another recess was ordered.

In the seventh hour of negotiation an agreement was finally reached, pending ratification by the KKP in Gdansk: The government would dismiss all persons directly responsible for the beatings, after an investigation; antiriot police squads would be withdrawn from Bydgoszcz; a parliamentary commission would study the question of registration for Rural Solidarity.

Facing television cameras outside the Council of Ministers building, Solidarity Vice-Chairman Andrezej Gwiazda told the nation, "Tomorrow we go to work."

At an evening press conference, Walesa proclaimed the agreement a 70 percent success. "There will be objections," Walesa sighed prophetically, well aware of the trouble he faced back at the KKP in Gdansk.

A KKP meeting was convened late in the afternoon the following day, Tuesday, inside the conference hall at the Lenin Shipyard in Gdansk.

A letter arrived from Bydgoszcz union chairman Jan Rulewski, still in the hospital, denouncing Walesa's autocratic behavior, accusing him of losing everything and calling the agreement a "dishonor" to the union.

More incensed was Rural Solidarity's twenty-three-year-old leader, Jan Kulaj, who accused Walesa of selling out the farmers' cause. Kulaj insisted that the KKP not ratify the agreement.

Walesa confronted the fury head on, reminding farmers that they had not notified the KKP before starting their strike in Bydgoszcz. He argued that Rural Solidarity could not expect to be registered overnight and that the agreement at least set the stage for further talks between farmers and the government. The "eggheads" supported Walesa. Radical KKP members turned their anger toward the "eggheads," accusing them of manipulation and of confusing the membership with legal jargon.

Walesa presented a letter from twenty-two regional Solidarity branches endorsing the agreement.

Tempers were quelled and reason prevailed. Following a short recess a vote was taken: twenty-five yes, four no, and six abstentions. The agreement was ratified.

12.

Hardliner Objections

WITHIN DAYS of the agreement with the government, several Solidarity officials from the union's radical faction—most of them linked to KOR—resigned from the KKP. Radical Anna Walentynowicz was dropped from the Lenin Shipyard's union executive committee. But throughout Poland the agreement was met with relief. Although Polish workers had been ready to strike, they were aware of the high financial price the country would pay for such action.

Some tension and fear remained as Warsaw Pact maneuvers continued. Radio Free Europe and the BBC World Service reported a Soviet troop call-up. United States Defense Secretary Caspar Weinberger announced that Soviet troop movements were "consist-

ent with a move to go into Poland." The Swedes prepared a complex contingency plan of air and naval assistance for Polish refugees.

The Soviet and Eastern European press was in-
timidating. The Soviet Communist Party daily, *Pravda*,
blasted First Secretary Kania for knuckling under to
Solidarity. The Soviet government daily, *Izvestia*, reported that counterrevolutionary movements were
becoming more brazen in Poland. The East German
press declared that East Germans "must be ready and
capable of firmly defending the socialist homeland with
weapons." At a Czechoslovakian Communist Party
congress in mid-April Party chief Gustav Husak warned
that Eastern European countries would not remain passive if any threat to Poland's socialist system developed.
Soviet Communist Party chief Leonid Brezhnev, present at the congress, eased the tension by affirming his
belief that the Polish leadership would be able to "oppose the designs of enemies of socialism."

On April 1 meat rationing was again introduced, this
time on an open-ended basis. But the rationing did not
alleviate the long food lines that had become commonplace since Christmas. Indeed, the situation was made
worse by inept local authority management of ration
coupons.

Shoppers would begin to line up on the streets outside food shops as early as 2:00 A.M., a good six hours
before the shops opened their doors and even longer
before the shops received their delivery of goods. Shop-

ping had become a full-time occupation—even a profession. Some Poles took part-time jobs standing in queues for others.

In Bydgoszcz a former district governor and a police chief were arrested for embezzlement of public funds. Already criminal investigations were being conducted against four former government ministers, eight deputy ministers, six district secretaries, seven district governors, and other officials numbering nearly two hundred.

The first issue of the long-awaited *Solidarity Weekly* hit the streets on April 3 and quickly sold out its print run of half a million. A week later Prime Minister Jaruzelski, in accord with the government's agreement with Solidarity, requested parliament to declare a sixty-day ban on strikes and parliament complied. The KKP responded from Gdansk with a short statement: "No resolution of parliament will prevent a strike if the security of our union is threatened or an unacceptable violation of the law occurs." But the union's moderate leadership was not displeased.

In mid-April Solidarity released a forty-five-page draft program on the union's future activities. One proposal recommended the establishment of worker self-management at factories. The program stressed that Solidarity's presence was the main guarantee of democratic renewal in Poland and that "we should be determined, and prepared for sacrifice," in building a more democratic society.

The draft was strongly attacked by the Party's hard-liner-controlled newspapers. The assumption that Solidarity, and only Solidarity, could guarantee democratic changes in Poland did not please the Party leadership, who believed itself the guiding light of Polish daily life.

An agreement was reached in Bydgoszcz on April 16 on the issue of Rural Solidarity:

1. The government would draft a special bill in parliament as a legal basis for registration of a farmers' union.
2. Farmers' representatives would work with a parliamentarian commission on the bill's details.
3. A farmers' union would be officially registered by May 10.
4. The farmers' union would be consulted on every parliamentary bill or government decree pertaining to agriculture.

The farmers, in return, would declare in writing their recognition of the Communist Party's leading role in Poland and promise never to organize a political party. The farmers also agreed to a name change: First Secretary Kania had stated repeatedly that Rural Solidarity could not exist in socialist Poland. But Kania never said that the "Independent Self-governed Trade Union of Individual Farmers" could not exist. (Nevertheless, Poles continued to refer to the farmers' union as Rural Solidarity.)

Near the end of April, KKP Co-Vice-Chairman Bogdan Lis met with a government delegation to discuss Solidarity's international activities. The government expressed concern and claimed that some foreign organizations that had aided Solidarity were fronts for Western intelligence agencies. Lis affirmed the union's sensitivity about such charges and assured the delegation of the care Solidarity exercised in accepting gifts. (In fact, Solidarity activists were busy enough with their own problems without worrying about from whom they received aid.)

May Day 1981 in Poland was far different from any May Day of the past. Traditionally, it was a day of parades in which workers marched if they valued their jobs; a day during which the Communist Party displayed its power. But in 1981 there was no Party pomp. Solidarity's KKP declared May 1 a workers' holiday and advised all workers to spend the day as they pleased.

The first of May also saw new rationing for butter, flour, and rice. The government announced that beginning June 1 semolina, milk powder, and soap powder would also be rationed.

On May 9 Walesa and a Solidarity delegation, which included Warsaw chief Zbigniew Bujak and Bydgoszcz chairman Jan Rulewski, flew to Tokyo at the invitation of Sohyo, the Japanese trade union council. In the memory book at a museum in Nagasaki, the site of atomic destruction in 1945, Walesa wrote, "How could you do this, Man?"

On May 12 the Independent Self-governed Trade Union of Individual Farmers was legally registered at

the Supreme Court in Warsaw. Three million farmers
—85 percent of all the farmers in Poland—had already
signed up for membership. Emotion-charged speeches
and song filled the air outside the courthouse. A telegram arrived from Walesa: "Here in friendly Japan, we
are with you. God bless you."

The farmers' jubilation was cut short the next day,
May 13, at 5:17 P.M. when pistol shots rang out in St.
Peter's Basilica, Rome. Popular radio disc jockey Andrzej Turski interrupted his radio program with an announcement, his voice cracking with emotion: "I do not
want to receive such news, ever in my life. . . . The pope
was shot in Rome."

Shock and disbelief spread across Poland as details of
the shooting were broadcast on radio and television. In
Warsaw, fifty thousand persons congregated in front of
Warsaw Castle in the Old Town for a special mass.
Theaters and movie houses were closed, television and
radio programs canceled.

From the autumn day in 1978 when Cardinal Wojtyla
was elected pope, the pontiff became the number-one
authority in Poland. After many years of Communist
rule, the Poles regained their national, social, and religious dignity. They rallied around their Polish pope
with renewed spirit.

And when Pope John Paul II visited his homeland in
June 1979 millions of Poles took to the streets to welcome him. The Polish people were struck then by the
realization that the whole nation felt the same way

about the pope; that the atheistic Communist Party was indeed a minority, they the majority. Even long-standing Party members came out of the closet to welcome the pontiff.

Now, two years on, Poland was united in its grief. Walesa, in Japan when he learned of the shooting, made his way to the nearest church for prayer.

The country came out of shock when news arrived that the pope would recover, but sadness and prayers continued for Cardinal Wyszynski who lay, everyone knew, on his deathbed.

At 4:40 A.M. on May 28 Cardinal Wyszynski died. The seventy-nine-year-old primate had ruled the Polish Catholic Church for nearly thirty years. The Church, under Wyszynski's leadership, was the spiritual force behind Solidarity, and Wyszynski himself Solidarity's most effective intermediary in negotiation with the government.

Thousands of Poles filed past the simple wooden coffin in White Friar's Church for three days and nights to pay their last respects. The cardinal's funeral was conducted on Sunday afternoon, May 31, and televised live to the nation. Nearly a half million people took part in a mourning mass, celebrated in Polish by Vatican Secretary of State Agostino Cardinal Casaroli. Wyszynski's body was laid to rest in the crypt at Saint John's Cathedral. A thirty-day mourning period of prayer and social peace was declared by the Church.

The next day Walesa flew to Geneva with a Solidarity

delegation for a conference of the International Labor Organization. He was accorded a hero's welcome. In his address to the ILO assembly of nearly two thousand labor leaders, Walesa warned against foreign interference in the social transformation process in Poland.

"I wish to declare from this international platform to all the people and all the countries of the world," announced Walesa, "that the Poles are capable of settling their internal affairs by themselves." The Soviet delegation to the labor congress sat in awkward silence while the rest of the assembly stood and cheered.

At a Central Committee plenary session on June 11, Party hardliners lashed out at First Secretary Kania for conceding too much, they said, to Solidarity. A new vote for Party leadership was proposed, but defeated after several generals voiced their support of Kania.

Walesa, back from Switzerland, set off on a cross-country tour of Poland to quell growing radicalism in the union. When Walesa spoke at a soccer stadium in Lublin, unidentified elements desecrated a monument honoring Soviet soldiers who had liberated Lublin during the Second World War, by bombarding it with white paint. It was not the first of such provocations. In late May another monument to Soviet soldiers had been vandalized with white paint. Journalist Association president Stefan Bratkowski warned that only the hardliners "would welcome the prospect of Soviet intervention and would not be opposed to provoking it."

Walesa condemned the vandalism and offered to

clean the monument himself. (The paint was eventually removed by Lublin union members and city firemen.)

"Let's give the government a chance to rule," became Walesa's theme. His campaign to curb the union's radical faction was moderately successful. The distinction between Solidarity and KOR was becoming sharper each day.

In late June the Party began preparations for the Extraordinary Party Congress scheduled for July 14 through 18. Rank-and-file Party members had deluged the Central Committee with demands for an "extra" congress since the birth of Solidarity (Party congresses are normally convened every four years). Most of the three million Party members were workers, with one million of them belonging to Solidarity. The Party was no longer the monolithic, iron-fisted institution it had been in the past. The rank and file, forgotten in the turmoil brought about by Solidarity, responded by reexamining their own beliefs and organizing their own new structure. They built a network of local Party interenterprise committees known as the "horizontal structure." This new movement was born in Gdansk, the Solidarity stronghold, but quietly mushroomed in the other large industrial cities. The movement's activists aimed to alter the Party structure; to institute secret ballots, nominations from the floor, and limited terms of office for Party officials—reforms unheard of in Eastern Bloc countries. According to polls published in Poland in the spring of 1981, 99 percent of the Party's rank-and-file membership were in favor of fundamental changes within the Party structure.

The impact of the horizontal structure's "social-democratic revisionism" alarmed the Party hardliners. There existed no precedent for such reform in any socialist country. Most outspoken over the new movement was top Party hardliner Stefan Olszowski. (In early spring Olszowski had been appointed chairman of the Congress Commission, the body that would organize the Extraordinary Congress.)

"The Party must remain the Party," Olszowski declared on national television, "and not become a discussion club." But the Party's rank and file desired more discussion and greater freedom of speech. And despite Olszowski's grip on the Party's communication channels, the horizontal structure got the word out through leaflets and booklets—with the assistance of Solidarity!

The hardliners countered the movement by forming their own groups, known as forums. The first such forum was established in the Silesian capital, Katowice. Another was created in Poznan. Both issued statements attacking the new liberal trends in the Party and accused First Secretary Kania of failing to crack down on both the unions and the "revisionists."

From across the country 1964 delegates were elected to attend the Party congress. Twenty percent of the delegates held dual membership in both the Party and Solidarity.

The Party congress was convened in an atmosphere

of excitement. Intensive lobbying and political ma-
neuvering filled the labyrinth of corridors in the Stalin-
esque Palace of Culture and Science in downtown Warsaw. Each political faction attempted to discredit the
other. The hardliners distributed a letter allegedly written by former First Secretary Gomulka accusing First
Secretary Kania of participating in the decision to call
in troops against the shipyard strikers in Gdansk in
1970. (The letter was a fake.)

Deputy Premier Rakowski, a man known for playing
all sides depending on the political climate, delivered
an emotional speech to the congress warning of a
bloodbath if any of the liberal reforms of the past
twelve months were reversed.

Congressional delegates expelled seven former top
officials from the Party for incompetence, corruption,
and mismanagement, including former First Secretary
Gierek.

A list of candidates for membership in the new Central Committee was prepared. It was decided that the
Committee would expand from 142 to 200 positions.
There were to be 275 candidates, a radical departure
from the old system whereby Party appointees were
screened and selected *before* the start of a congress.
Moreover, votes would be taken by secret ballot, yet
another precedent. The Party leaderships of Eastern
European countries could only look on in horror.

Stanislaw Kania won easy reelection as first secretary.
Leading hardliners Tadeusz Grabski and Andrzej

Zabinski were not so lucky; they were dropped from the Central Committee.

The Party congress overshadowed another important event. On July 7 Pope John Paul II named Archbishop Jozef Glemp the new Polish primate. Glemp, a protégé of Cardinal Wyszynski, was known as a specialist in both canon and civil law.

At his first press conference Glemp assured the country that he would follow the road paved by Wyszynski. Four days after his appointment the new primate met with Prime Minister Jaruzelski, signaling the continuance of a close relationship between the Church and the government.

On July 23 the government announced tighter meat rationing and promptly triggered new social unrest. Poles were becoming increasingly fed up with long food lines, which had become commonplace for everything from food staples to cigarettes and alcohol, which by this time were also rationed. The government also announced plans to raise food prices by up to 400 percent. This sparked off "hunger marches" in many Polish cities. Workers suspected that food was being secretly stockpiled by the authorities.

On the last day of July, a delegation from Warsaw's Solidarity branch visited parliament to request quick action in dealing with food black marketeering and food wastage. Parliament offered no remedy, so the union's Warsaw branch called a strike alert, to begin Monday morning, August 3.

The government dispatched an invitation to the KKP in Gdansk for urgent talks on the intended strike alert. Its timing was poor. Walesa was in the hospital on doctor's orders, suffering from exhaustion. Solidarity's vice chairman, Andrzej Gwiazda, answered the government's invitation with a telex stating that due to "technical matters" talks could not take place before August 3. That night the Polish News Agency reported the rejection. Walesa defied his doctors and immediately led a union delegation to Warsaw.

The talks began on the morning of August 3 at the Council of Ministers building. A mile away, outside the Central Committee building, a demonstration over food shortages began. It took the form of a motorcade, made up of hundreds of taxis and private cars. Drivers blared their horns as they passed the gray, fortresslike Committee building. When bus and truck drivers attempted to join the motorcade, the flow of traffic toward the building was halted by police. Drivers retaliated by blocking the capital's main traffic junction, refusing to budge until permitted to follow the motorcade's route. By midafternoon most of Warsaw's traffic was at a standstill, hopelessly snarled. Banners on the buses and trucks read: "A Hungry Nation Can Eat Its Rulers."

The government-KKP talks resolved nothing. Walesa spoke out in favor of the protesting drivers, announcing that their demonstration should continue until Wednesday.

The traffic pileup of over 150 buses and trucks took on a carnival spirit. One bus was converted into a canteen, another a first-aid station, and so on. Drivers bedded down in their vehicles for the night.

The government-KKP talks were resumed on August 6. Deputy Premier Rakowski angrily took exception to Solidarity's interest in the problem of adequate food production and distribution. It was, Rakowski argued, a political matter in which the union should not concern itself.

Walesa reiterated his stance that Solidarity would best be able to convince the country that food was not deliberately being stockpiled if representatives from the union could monitor food production and distribution.

Rakowski would have none of it, and he presented the union delegation with a list of government demands, including a call for a ban on strikes, an endorsement of the government's plan to raise food prices, and a withdrawal from its campaign for worker self-management.

Walesa sarcastically asked just what Solidarity was *permitted* to do. The meeting ended in disagreement. Polish editors received an order from the main press office, controlled by hardliner Stefan Olszowski, to report negatively on Solidarity's role in the talks. Indignant journalists protested the order. One hundred and fifty radio journalists drafted and signed an open letter to their listeners exposing the hardliner media mani-

When other leaders failed to check Solidarity and Walesa, the Soviets and the Polish Communist Party reached into the army to do the job. The man they chose was General Jaruzelski, here meeting with Soviet leader Leonid Brezhnev in Moscow in March of 1982.

Jaruzelski opening a session of the Polish parliament. Above
him is speaker of the parliament, Stanislaw Gucwa.

Jaruzelski called out his troops and martial law was declared throughout Poland just before Christmas 1981. In this photograph a line of police confronts demonstrators on a snow-covered street in Warsaw.

Through the long winter the Polish people kept an uneasy truce with the Polish Army. In May of 1982 they spilled out into the streets shouting, "Long live Solidarity."

Opposite: But the Army and the police fought back against their own people. In Warsaw and other cities the troops used water cannons and tear gas to disperse the people. Thousands of others were arrested and put into detention camps.

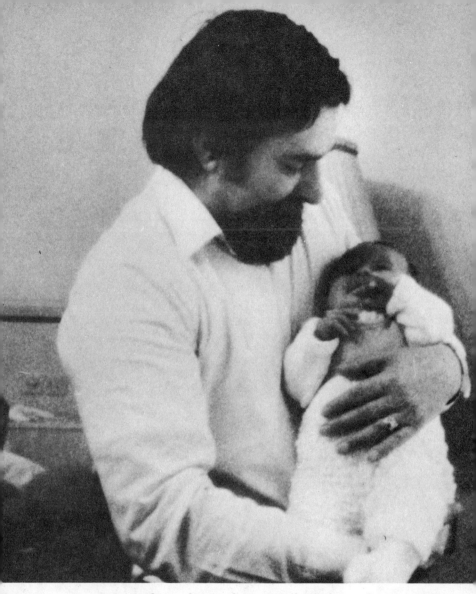

Among those detained was Lech Walesa, the man who shouted, "I declare a strike!" and who for sixteen months led a movement that shocked the communists but thrilled the rest of the world. In this photograph, taken for ABC's "World News Tonight," Walesa is shown in detention holding his infant daughter, Victoria Maria, during a brief visit by his wife.

pulation. In addition, a Polish Journalist Association task force prepared an in-depth study on the subject. Both documents were published in *Solidarity Weekly.*

The long-running feud between Stefan Olszowski and Journalist Association President Stefan Bratkowski flared into all-out war. When printers called a strike two weeks later to protest hardliner manipulation, Bratkowski refused to mediate, as was his custom. The effectiveness of the two-day printers' strike dealt a heavy blow to Party morale and resulted in an informal alliance between journalists and Solidarity. Walesa called on all Polish journalists to report the truth about Solidarity's successes.

"If this leads to reprisals we shall protect you," he asserted.

13.

The Darkness Returns

THREE MONTHS before General Wojciech Jaruzelski sent his army troops into the streets of Poland to reimpose the supremacy of the Communist Party, Lech Walesa, the little man with the pipe and the bushy moustache, stood before an audience in the Olivia Sports Arena in Gdansk. The date was September 5, 1981, and he was speaking to Solidarity's first national congress. There were 892 delegates at the congress and they represented 9,457,584 Solidarity members from 38 branches.

"We are here at the will of those who elect us—the working people of all Poland," Walesa said. "Each of us individually does not count much. Together we are the strength of the millions who constitute Solidarity." He added: "We shall open a vista for a better Poland only if we act in solidarity. The struggle is going to be long and hard, but we shall win and we shall make Poland a country of our dreams."

A Solidarity program was drafted, to be discussed at each branch of Solidarity and every large factory work force before its final approval at the second round of the congress later in the month.

In a move influenced mostly by radical KOR-affiliated delegates, Solidarity pledged its support for free trade unions throughout Eastern Europe, causing no small amount of Communist fury and verbal abuse.

In the space between the two rounds of congress, Walesa caused an uproar among Solidarity's radicals when he, with three of his closest associates, made a decision without consulting regional union leaders to accept a government compromise on the issue of worker self-management (the government would appoint managers in some enterprises, Solidarity would appoint managers in others). Many regional union leaders were furious with the compromise and with the dictatorial manner in which Walesa acted. But Walesa maintained he was being realistic and only carrying out his leadership mandate.

In New York City, Solidarity opened, or seemed to open, its first foreign bureau. The office, "wholly independent and self-governing," was initiated with financial aid from the American AFL-CIO. Radio Moscow responded with a claim that the CIA was behind Solidarity's United States information bureau. This prompted discussion at the second round of Solidarity's congress in late September as to whom in Solidarity had sponsored a New York office and for what reason. No one owned up. Even Walesa claimed no knowledge of the office. Solidarity, New York, quietly shut down its operations on October 30.

On the second day of the second round of Solidarity's congress, September 27, Walesa was officially reprimanded by union delegates for practicing "Napoleonism" and for approving an agreement with the government on behalf of Solidarity without the union's full backing. Still, and despite official censure, Walesa was reelected with ease on October 2 as chairman of Solidarity. More important, eleven of the twelve elected positions on Solidarity's governing presidium were filled with Walesa nominees, thus according Walesa a full mandate to rule for two years.

"I can only ride on the horses you have given me," Walesa told the delegates.

During the congress KOR officially dissolved itself, thereby diminishing the radical influence inside Solidarity, albeit only temporarily.

On October 18 an event occurred that would have far-reaching implications for those inside the Olivia Sports Arena. Stanislaw Kania, who had tried to reach compromises with Walesa while keeping the Soviet Union out of Polish affairs, was ousted as leader of the Communist Party and replaced by Prime Minister Jaruzelski. The decision was taken by the Party's Central Committee at a stormy meeting in Warsaw. In dismissing Kania the Central Committee ominously made clear its distaste for the gains made by Solidarity and the reduced influence of the Communist Party. In a resolution, the Committee referred to what it called "existing dangers to the existence of the state." This dangerous activity by "antisocialists," the Committee added, might require the government to implement "its constitutional prerogatives to guarantee peace in the country." This, of course, meant the imposition of martial law, and what better man was there to do so than Jaruzelski? Finally, the Committee asked that the government renegotiate its agreements with Solidarity, reimpose the six-day work week, and suspend the right of workers to strike, at least temporarily.

In Washington, the State Department expressed concern over the Committee's resolution, saying that the United States saw "no reason for martial law in Poland." But in Gdansk the news from Warsaw was greeted with surprising passivity. "He is a soldier and I like soldiers," Walesa is known to have said about Jaruzelski.

Walesa's calm observation seemed to be echoed elsewhere in Poland and, indeed, in many other places around the world. Jaruzelski was viewed as a "moderate" who would get along with Solidarity, even though he might disagree with its goals and if only to keep Poland's problems out of the hands of the Soviets. This "moderate" view was based on how Jaruzelski had reacted to two previous events in Poland. In 1970, when Wladyslaw Gomulka had requested the use of troops to end riots on the Baltic coast, Jaruzelski had withdrawn his support of the Communist leader, and Gomulka had lost his job. In 1976 rioting again occurred and the Party asked him to use his troops to restore order. Jaruselski replied, "Polish troops will never be used to fire upon Polish workers." In a few months Walesa and other Solidarity leaders would recall that reply with bitterness. The legend of Jaruzelski would not last.

With Jaruzelski in charge, Poland began to lean toward a government of national unity, comprised of Church, union, and state. The future suddenly looked bright and Walesa canceled a visit he had been planning to the United States. (He had intended to fly in and out of Canada, thus avoiding United States air space in sympathy with American air traffic control strikers.)

On November 4 a historic "domestic summit" was convened in Warsaw. Jaruzelski, Archbishop Glemp, and Walesa came face to face for preliminary discussion on a proposed Front of National Accord. Official talks opened two weeks later to formulate a "front of national unity."

But hopes for a united effort to solve Poland's problems proved futile when Solidarity's leadership refused to accept new government bills on economic reform. At this point, Solidarity's radicals were interested in nothing less than a share of political power.

At a Communist Party Central Committee meeting

on November 28, Jaruzelski was urged to take emergency powers if necessary and "tidy things up."

Perhaps to signal his Party critics, and Solidarity, of his resolve to stand tough, Jaruzelski dispatched riot police to break up a sit-in strike of fire brigade cadets in Warsaw on December 2. For the first time since March, force was used against striking workers.

Solidarity's leaders responded with a strike alert and they gathered in Radom for an emergency meeting. In a closed session, Walesa accused the government of cheating. He also lamented, in an effort to appease Solidarity's radicals, that "confrontation [with the government] is inevitable." Walesa was red-faced when, several days later, the government broadcast his imprudent remark over the radio. His words had been secretly tape-recorded by a government mole inside the union.

At Solidarity's final formal meeting on Saturday, December 12—in the same Gdansk hall where it had been born sixteen months earlier—the union, now clearly in the hands of the radicals (Walesa said little), decided to call for a national referendum on whether or not Poland's Communist government should be replaced by a provisional one. It was Solidarity's strongest challenge yet.

Union delegates traded black jokes about possible arrest as they dispersed into the cold night air. Hours later most of them were in jail. Darkness had returned to Poland.

14.

Epilogue

As the final words of this book are written, Lech Walesa is still in detention, held incommunicado by the Polish government, which arrested him on that Sunday morning in December of 1981. Reports from Poland indicate that a Solidarity underground is active within the country, keeping alive the spirit of freedom that Walesa proclaimed on that crucial day in 1980 when he cried out to fellow workers in Gdansk, "I declare a strike!" Other reports show that millions of workers have not lost their will to resist the Communist Party, and that they are ready to strike again for their independence. Whatever happens in the future, it is evident that the impact of Solidarity's sixteen months was huge throughout Poland, from the largest cities to

the smallest villages. Politically, socially, and economi-
cally, Poland will never again be the same country.
What occurred at the Lenin Shipyard in Gdansk in
August 1980 was an inevitable eruption. Like a volcano,
pressure had been building up among Poland's laborers
through three decades of Communist mismanagement
and repression.

In the early 1950s it was a crime for Poles to listen to
foreign radio broadcasts, possess foreign currency, or
criticize Communist rulers. One could lose one's job for
attending church. Stefan Wyszynski, then a bishop, was
bound under house arrest during the Stalinist years.

Ironically, this repression resulted in the keen appreciation that generations of Poles developed for their
history, culture, and language, and a keen sense of their
national unity. They are a proud, patriotic people, and
fiercely independent.

The roots of the workers' revolt date back to 1956
when workers in Poznan rioted for "bread and freedom." They were beaten back by Polish police, but the
progression for change began there. As a result of the
riots, the Communist Party's leadership was purged.
Wladyslaw Gomulka, imprisoned during Stalin's reign
in Russia, was elected first secretary. Gomulka promised a "Polish way to socialism," expelling Soviet advisers from the country and purging the Polish armed
forces of Soviet officers. The Soviets under Khrushchev
eased their tight grip on Poland, but the country remained under absolute state control. The state badly

mismanaged Poland's enormous potential for a prosperous economy. Factory and enterprise managers
were chosen for their Party affiliations, not for their
capabilities and qualifications. ("Inactive, mediocre,
but loyal," went the joke.) Family farms were reluc-
tantly tolerated, but were not assisted.

In 1970 Gomulka attempted to rest the Party's economic failures on the shoulders of the workers by rais-
ing food prices. This triggered the bloody riots and
Gomulka's subsequent downfall. Edward Gierek rose
to power on a platform of promises to bring innovation
into Poland's political and economic life. The standard
of living did improve, the innovation being hefty loans
from Western banks. But the loans were misused, and
by 1975 Gierek's economy was in a shambles. Sensing
trouble, the innovative Gierek launched a campaign in
the media of "happy face" propaganda. Newspapers
published only good news and television broadcast
smiling faces. New factories were ceremoniously
opened on time for the benefit of television cameras,
despite being months away from completion. Poles
were treated to a grand façade of economic success.

The burden of state inefficiency and deception was
again laid on the workers, resulting in the revolt of
1976. Gierek looked again to Western banks for a solution and received more credit. In exchange for these
loans, Poland was expected to buy goods from Western
companies, and more often than not Poland became a
dump for Western products. The kickbacks made Party

leaders wealthy. The workers were not so lucky.

Party leaders, content and secluded in their luxury villas, were not aware, did not wish to be aware, of the workers' unrest. District Party officials tried to report the growing unrest to their superiors, but their diligence resulted in reprimands. Didn't they see the happy faces on television news each night? The people are happy and don't you dare think otherwise! Many local Party officials began to fake their reports, and public opinion polls also were invented, their authors wishing to remain in good standing with the Party leadership.

In November 1978 an independent think tank made up of Party members, scholars, journalists, Church officials, and the intelligentsia was formed in Warsaw. Experience and the Future (DiP), as it was called, paved the way for Solidarity's existence. Initially organized by top Party officials in response to growing intelligentsia sympathy for dissident movements, DiP's first session was so stormy that the Party immediately tried to disband the group. The think tank went underground. Members met covertly and prepared two detailed reports. The first, published in May 1979, shattered Gierek's "happy-face" façade. It bluntly exposed the inefficiency of Gierek's regime and the government's blunders and miscalculations in dealing with the economy.

DiP's second report, distributed in April 1980, was a discourse on Poland's socioeconomic situation titled,

"How Can We Come Out of It?" In this report, the think tank predicted an eruption of social revolt within two years. In essence, experience and the future taught workers to understand the link between poor living conditions and the political and economic system of mismanagement and corruption in the country. The workers were eager to learn, and their new awareness of the cause of Poland's ailing economy festered, grew stronger, was restricted, expanded, and finally blew up when meat prices were raised on July 1, 1980.

A third DiP report was published on August 22, 1980, and distributed to Party leaders. Titled "Where Should We Start?" the three-page report recommended that the country's leadership take the following steps:

1. Present the nation with a full report on Poland's internal situation
2. Recognize the workers' right for independent representation
3. Recognize the workers' right to strike
4. Recognize freedom of religious belief, without discrimination
5. Guarantee equal rights for non-Party members
6. Curb censorship
7. Democratize the Communist Party

Several months after Solidarity was formed a legitimate poll conducted by the Polish Academy of Science revealed that 89.1 percent of all Poles supported the union without reservations. Another poll reported that only the Church was more trusted than Solidarity by the Polish people. The Party ranked last, behind fourteen other institutions.

Most visible of Solidarity's impact was its effect on the Polish media. By late October 1980 the union had organized its own telex network, Agency Solidarity, which distributed union news to all Solidarity branches.

In its struggle against official censorship, Solidarity found an ally in journalists weary of being ordered what, and what not, to report. Government censorship was, of course, not limited to strikes and social unrest. Reads one government circular on censorship: "All statistics of safety and hygiene at work, or occupational hazards, must be withheld."

In September 1980 defiant journalists throughout Poland demanded a congress of their journalist association. Convened in late October, the congress elected liberal Stefan Bratkowski its president. Under Bratkowski's new leadership the association stressed the importance of the media's neutrality. Party hardliners were incensed. Communist Party doctrine dictates that the media be a key instrument of Party power (Lenin's utterance about the power of the printing press is well heeded). Hardliners were consoled only by their control over the distribution of newsprint paper. When a popular weekly magazine for managers published a series of articles on worker self-management, it suddenly found itself suffering an acute newsprint shortage.

Solidarity effected considerable impact on the Polish Communist Party, known as the Polish United Workers' Party. The Party emerged from the August 1980 strike wave in virtual disintegration, its authority shattered. It was viewed by the public as having driven the country into national bankruptcy through miscalculation and a policy of lies and deception.

By February the internal Party struggle between the hardliners, moderates, and liberals was in full swing. Hardliners wished to withdraw from the Gdansk agreement, disband the union, and institute economic reforms without outside (non-Party) influence; liberals wished to democratize the Party, institute full economic reform, and establish worker self-management, thus lessening the Party's power; moderates believed in the aims of the liberals, but wished to realize these aims in gradual steps without demeaning the Party's authority. There had never existed such distinct and harsh division within the Party's membership.

On the Party grass-roots level, the horizontal structure was on the upswing, attempting its own democratic reform of the Party. It stirred panic within the Party machine, the Nomenklatura, when it first surfaced in the spring of 1981. It was the horizontal structure that was most responsible for democratic reforms at the Extraordinary Party Congress the following July, including secret ballots and limited terms of office for Party officials. But even with these new reforms, the Party's credibility did not improve.

In the short term, Solidarity wrought havoc on the Polish economy. Frequent strikes worsened an already acute problem. Production had fallen far short of projected aims, particularly in the areas of coal and agriculture. As inflation skyrocketed, full rationing did not deal effectively with drastic shortages (Polish currency and ration coupons were plentiful; goods were not).

Food shortages were a result of a fatuous government agricultural policy whereby independent farmers, who supply 80 percent of the nation's food, had for years been discriminated against in favor of the far less efficient state-owned farms. Family-managed farms could not buy modern agricultural machinery and were permitted to procure only limited amounts of coal, building materials, and tools.

The food shortages led to the widespread rumor that the government had secretly stockpiled foodstuffs outside of Poland. Railway workers in eastern Poland discovered food transports disguised as machinery parts. Food shipments sent to Poland by Western charity organizations were routinely blocked by the Ministry of Foreign Commerce. West Germany had difficulty getting powdered milk allowed into Poland for infants; United States butter was "disqualified" because of its "fat percentage." The former Polish ambassador to Japan, Zdzislaw Rurarz, spoke of difficulty he had in getting Warsaw to accept rice offered by the Japanese. After defecting to the United States following the imposition of martial law, Rurarz said he believed the

Polish government's strategy had been "the worse the better." It is curious that immediately following the imposition of martial law Polish shops were flooded with meat and other goods that had not been seen for months.

Solidarity's social impact can perhaps be best examined by assessing the change it effected on the small Polish town.

Wysokie Mazowieckie, the birthplace of the author's paternal grandparents, lies eighty miles northeast of Warsaw, not far from the Soviet border. It is a sleepy agricultural community with a population of approximately fifty-five hundred.

Like everywhere else in Poland, Wysokie was plagued with drastic shortages when the author visited the town in July 1981. The only restaurant in town had no food, only tea. More than 75 percent of its business was conducted through bartering, a system popularly known as "friends-connections."

Wysokie's farmers farm without fertilizer, pesticides, cement, steel, wood, or machinery. In 1980 they were in a crisis situation. Their wheat harvest was catastrophic; their potato harvest down by 75 percent, and they produced only one-half their normal quota of sugar beets. Despite their excellent soil, agricultural factories were never built in Wysokie. Polish patriots fought Soviet soldiers in the forests around Wysokie until 1951 and, consequently, Wysokie and its neighboring towns have been refused state funds ever since.

Theirs is a punished area.

But almost incredibly, morale in Wysokie was strong. Its Solidarity branch had been formed in October 1980. It had a nine-member Executive Committee, and half of Wysokie's population had become members.

Before then, the local Party administration had run everything in Wysokie. Corruption was widespread among the privileged Party elite. The union openly challenged that system. If someone was unfairly dismissed from their job, as was a hospital nurse who refused to permit a Party bigwig to cut into a line for treatment, Solidarity intervened.

Explained an official of Wysokie's church, himself a union member: "The Party governs the stomach [it controls jobs and wages]; the Church governs the soul; Solidarity tries to minimize the Party's governance of the stomach."

The union's most active campaign in Wysokie had been to combat alcoholism, one of Poland's foremost social problems. In June 1981 the local Solidarity executive demanded the authorities shut down a notorious tavern known as Szatan (Devil's Bar). By August Szatan had been converted to a milk bar.

The union's executive demanded that the ground floor and basement of the local Party building be transformed into a kindergarten. The Party acquiesced with barely a whimper, fearful of a strike.

Another union project was the resurrection of an important monument in Wysokie's main square. Erected originally in 1928 to commemorate ten years of Polish independence, the monument had been torn down and buried in the town square during the Stalin era. Inspired by the new freedom Solidarity assured them, Wysokie's citizens had become intent on "digging up the history of Poland."

Members of Wysokie's community, like Poles everywhere, laughed loud and hard at the suggestion of Soviet military intervention in Polish affairs. The Soviet Union, they pointed out, has its own problems with scattered strikes, civil unrest, not to mention Afghanistan. When a Solidarity banner was discovered early one morning wrapped around a statue of Lenin in the Russian town of Grodno, local Party authorities were not amused. They mounted a house-to-house search for the "antisocialist element." (Smuggled back issues of *Solidarity Weekly* and union buttons are hot items on the Soviet black market, fetching up to fifty dollars each.)

During the entire sixteen months that Solidarity confronted the Communist Party there were constant warnings by Western government officials and by Western reporters that the Soviet Union would send in its army to restore Poland to an acceptable Communist state. There were few people in Washington, London, or Paris who did not believe that the Russian Army was ready to cross the Polish border at the slightest indication that the leaders of Poland had lost control of the country. It was believed in some quarters that a Soviet invasion was put off only by the imposition of martial law by General Jaruzelski. But inside Poland, both the general public and the nation's leaders never believed that the Soviets (or worse still, their flunkies, the East Germans) would invade, nor do they believe it will ever happen. Their reasoning goes this way:

Economic: Soviet leaders do not wish COMECON to become burdened with Poland's $27-billion-dollar debt to Western banks nor risk the probability of a Western economic blockade and grain embargo (forty-three million metric tons of American grain was shipped to the Soviet Union in 1981, all of it badly needed).

Tactical: There is a very high probability that the Poles, including factions of the army and security forces, would fiercely resist an invasion, causing a bloody confrontation, followed by organized underground resistance.

Political: It is likely that a break would occur between the Soviet Communist Party and the Communist Parties of Western Europe.

The circumstances of Poland's internal strife in 1980 were quite different from those that prompted Soviet invasions of Hungary in 1956 and Czechoslovakia in 1968. The revolts of both countries were not worker rebellions, but were initiated by the respective leaders and intellectuals of the two countries; workers remained indifferent. More important, Hungary claimed neutrality and announced its intention to withdraw from the Warsaw Pact. Czechoslovakia intended to do the same. Poland's Solidarity movement never fostered such an ambition. Its leadership accepted the Soviet Union as Poland's natural ally.

The Soviet-Polish relationship may not be a marriage of love, but it remains a marriage of convenience. Betrayed by the Allies at Yalta, Poland itself has little intention of aligning itself with the West beyond friendship, even if she could. Poles continue to harbor an inherent distrust of the Germans, whether they are East Germans or West Germans.

"Germans traditionally march, and they like to march east," sums up one Polish Party official, perfectly serious. For centuries Russia tried to control Poland, Poles point out, but Germany wished to *annihilate* her. Poland feels safe against Germany with the Soviet Union as its neighboring, powerful ally.

Despite Poland's huge debts to Western banks and its dependence on economic assistance from the Soviet Union, Poland possesses the real potential to become a wealthy nation. Indeed, Western bankers would not have parted with such an enormous sum if Poland's economic potential did not warrant such attention.

Five percent of the world's silver is mined in Poland. Vast coal reserves—perhaps 120 billion tons of coal in the rich fields of Silesia—make Poland one of the largest coal exporters in the world. (It was the second largest coal exporter in 1979, after the United States.)

Most of Poland's land is fertile and arable for good farming and agriculture, and harbors great deposits of copper and sulphur. With proper management, Poland could become one of the more prosperous countries of Europe. Some observers have likened Poland's sense of tribal unity to that of Japan.

At the present time the Communist Party's influence and credibility have diminished considerably, perhaps even beyond repair. Hundreds of thousands of Poles have renounced their Party membership. It is questionable whether the Party will ever thoroughly dominate the country again. This very situation, coupled with the Church's important new influence on Polish affairs, is Solidarity's real lasting accomplishment.

Whether or not Solidarity is ever again officially recognized, the impact it—and a worker named Lech Walesa—exacted on Poland and its people are too strong to wash away. As one Pole put it, "You cannot cage a bird that has tasted freedom."